M000170293

THE ORVIS POCKET GUIDE TO
Great Lakes Salmon and Steelhead

THE ORVIS POCKET GUIDE TO
Great Lakes Salmon and Steelhead

Tips, Tactics, and Techniques
PLUS
Where To Fish and When

MATTHEW SUPINSKI

Photography by Matthew and Laurie Supinski
Illustrations by Jeff Kennedy

THE LYONS PRESS
Guilford, Connecticut
An imprint of The Globe Pequot Press

The Lyons Press is an imprint of The Globe Pequot Press.

10 9 8 7 6 5 4 3 2 1

Printed in Canada

Library of Congress Cataloging-in-Publication Data is available on file.

Supinski, Matthew.
   The Orvis pocket guide to Great Lakes salmon and steelhead / by
Matthew Supinski.
   p. cm.
  Includes index.
  ISBN 1-59228-205-9 (trade cloth)
   1. Salmon fishing—Great Lakes. 2. Steelhead fishing—Great Lakes.
3. Fly fishing—Great Lakes. I. Title. SH684.S856 2003
799.17'55—dc22

                        2003025455

CONTENTS

INTRODUCTION

A beautiful spring steelhead from Lake Michigan's Muskegon River.

It's through the sheer vastness of their cold, clear, azure waters that the inland seas of the Great Lakes draw us to them in a mysterious, mesmerizing fashion. With a volume of water large enough to flood the continental United States to a depth of 10 feet, I learned to respect their magnitude at an early age. Growing up on the thunderous Niagara Gorge, I stared in awe at its immense cascading flow, and I plied its waters with a rod and fly. Hour upon hour passed by as I fixated on the magic of feeling the "big pull" of the line. It was during these mystical moments, as the gushing waters hypnotized and immersed me into a surreal world, that I became a fly fisherman in pursuit of the elusive and charismatic sea-run fish. Salmon and steelhead fever has burned in my soul ever since. Today, through ingenious introductions of Pacific steelhead and salmon, along with restoring indigenous and creating new Atlantic salmon populations, the Great Lakes are numbered among the world's greatest salmonid fisheries.

THE STEELHEAD/SALMON INVASION

Dynasties are created by visionaries. Such was the case back in 1876 when William Fitzhugh, of Bay City, Michigan, and Seth Green of the Caledonia, New York fish hatchery, saw the potential that steelhead rainbow trout from California could find a new and prosperous home in the Great Lakes. With their initial planting in Michigan's Ausable River, a tributary to Lake Huron, by Fitzhugh and the U.S. Fish Commission's Northville Hatchery, along with Seth Green's stockings in the Caledonia Spring Creek/Genesee River tributary system of Lake Ontario, the steelhead infiltration of the lakes was well underway. By the 1900s, steelhead were introduced into Lakes Michigan, Erie, and Superior by all of the Great Lakes states and the province of Ontario. Rivers with cold, clear water and ample spawning gravel, such as Michigan's Pere Marquette, New York's Cattaraugus, Ontario's Saugeen, and other fertile rivers, saw wild steelhead populations established in their headwaters. From the early 1900s through the 1940s, plantings in all of the lakes with diverse strains of West

Coast steelhead continued as the foundation was laid and secured for the heritage of Great Lakes steelhead. The aggressive and heartier steelhead rainbows filled the biological niche for a riverine predator left vacant due to the demise of the native brook trout and grayling populations from logging, pollution, and habitat destruction.

As for Pacific salmon, it was ecological circumstance, followed by an experimental biological solution, that paved the way for their introduction. With the opening of the fourth Welland Canal in the 1930s, allowing ocean-going freighters to bypass the natural barrier of the Niagara River and make their way to the uppermost Lake Superior waters, exotic species were

Catch-and-release fly fishing has become an effective management tool on Great Lakes rivers.

introduced that created a negative and positive impact on the fishery. The salmonid predator, the lamprey, destroyed indigenous lake trout populations at an alarming rate by the 1940s. On the flip side, an incredibly reproducing ocean baitfish, the alewife, prospered without a natural predator to keep it in check. To combat the explosive alewife, Howard Tanner, of the Michigan DNR, brought the Pacific coho salmon to the northern waters of Lake Michigan's Platte Bay in the late 1960s. The salmon found a magnificent new foraging ground, and their wild and self-sustaining populations continue to prosper. With such a successful introduction, all the Great Lakes were stocked with this king of the food chain. Today, the Great Lakes are an angling mecca for chinook, coho, and pink Pacific salmon, as well as hatchery-raised and wild populations of steelhead. Coupled with the restoration of the once indigenous Atlantic salmon in Lake Ontario, along with the new and exciting fishery established for them in the St. Mary's River flowing into Lake Huron, the Great Lakes are a fisheries miracle. It has fused the Pacific and Atlantic salmonid fisheries in the heartland of America, a feat that continues to marvel all appreciative anglers.

How to Use this Book

We all somehow enter the world of big-game fly fishing from having pursued smaller yet extremely exciting quarry such as trout, panfish, and other gamefish. Or we may have experienced big gamefish from

The vast inland seas of the Great Lakes offer a wealth of cold, food-rich salmonid water.

the onset. I hope this text serves as an introductory tool for trout and small-game fly fishers to pursue Great Lakes salmon and steelhead with pragmatic ease. It is also intended to inspire additional analysis and perspective for seasoned Great Lakes anglers to become more proficient at their art.

Why do salmon and steelhead possess such enticing qualities to the fly angler? It all revolves around the meditation of the grab. It's in the big pull—the magnificent battles between angler and fish—the art and craft of the fly—and the elusive nature of these once sea-going beasts. Perhaps it begins on an early autumn, winter, or spring morning, as the tug of the river's flow glides gently around your waders. Your swinging fly or dead-drifted nymph is struck vehemently by a chrome-silver steelhead or massively girthed chinook or Atlantic salmon. Their cartwheeling jumps and driving runs send your reel's drag system into overload. During that moment, all of your thoughts and fears, all that you identify with in the real world of day-to-day life, vanishes from your mind during the spellbinding battle. You finally subdue your quarry and admire it, then you unhook it and send the beautiful voyager on its upstream journey. All the skill, reflexes, endurance, and savvy you possess as a fly fisher have been tested and sacrificed, and your reward was a fish of regal proportions. Here is where the ends justify the means. It is then that the addiction and lifelong journey of Great Lakes salmon and steelhead on a fly rod begins.

1

THE STEELHEAD/SALMON LIFECYCLE

Mike Dzienny shows off a hefty Michigan-strain winter steelhead from the Muskegon River.

The ocean-going strains of Pacific steelhead and salmon that now proliferate the Great Lakes, along with Atlantic salmon, have a very similar lifecycle. They all share the same need of foraging for prey in our inland seas, the return to their natal rivers to spawn and perpetuate the species, and the precarious lifecycle of the juvenile salmonids in the river ecosystem. Their amazing and courageous lifecycles have been admired since the dawn of man. The God-like elevation given to them by the Native Americans, and the barter value, equal to gold, given to the ocean-going Atlantic salmon by the conquering Roman legions of Gaul, has permanently established the noble status of these fish.

STEELHEAD

The steelhead rainbow trout (*Oncorhynchus mykiss*) is native to the entire Pacific basin from California to Alaska, and then around the Pacific rim of Russia. Since its introduction to the Great Lakes in 1876, it has adapted magnificently to the lakes' fertile rivers and ecosystems. An ocean-going steelhead and river-inhabiting rainbow trout are genetically identical. Only one life phase separates the two: the transformation from juvenile parr to sea-going smolt, which usually happens between the first and second year. Those strains of West Coast rainbows that were close enough to the ocean or had that slightest genetic disposition to run towards a big body of water became steelhead and passed on their predisposition for this behavior. Steelhead got their name from the dark grayish steel color of their heads and upper bodies with silver sides. During spawning, however, males display bright red side bands and have an iridescent quality, while the females show hues of pink and purple.

There are two genetic strains of steelhead: the winter and summer runs. The winter-strain fish begin entering the Great Lakes rivers as early as September, migrate upstream all fall and winter, and spawn in the spring. Unique Great Lakes wild winter strains have evolved in our rivers for over a century. The Little Manistee strain of Michigan, the Ganaraska of Ontario, the Bois Brule River of Wisconsin, the Thunder Bay Ontario streams of Lake Superior, and the wild strains of Ontario's Owen Sound and the north shore of Lake Erie represent unique genetic strains. The Chamber's Creek and Erie, Pennsylvania, corridor winter strains are very popular stocked strains in the Great Lakes. The average size of winter-strain fish is

This chrome-silver summer steelhead was taken from Lake Michigan's St. Joseph River.

between 4 and 10 pounds, with some fish achieving 20-pound-plus trophy status.

The Skamania summer strain, brought from the Washougal River of Washington in 1968 to Lake Michigan, run primarily from June through September in their initial phase and trickle in all fall and winter until their late January/February spawning period. Since they were bred to be "three salt steelhead" (fish that will remain in the big lake or ocean three years prior to spawning), they can achieve a massive 20 to 30 pounds. The current Great Lakes record is a 31-pound steelhead of Indiana-stocked Skamania strain taken from Lake Michigan.

Steelhead are prized for their extremely aggressive nature, willingness to take an assortment of fly presentations, and spectacular fighting and leaping ability—not to mention their extremely beautiful mix of silver, gray, and pastel body colors that are a feast for your eyes and your camera.

PACIFIC SALMON

Chinook, or king, salmon (*Oncorhynchus tshawytscha*) and coho, or silver, salmon (*Oncorhynkus kisutch*) are indigenous to the entire Pacific Rim from California through Alaska and Siberia and finally to the Sea of Japan. Brought to the Great Lakes in 1968 to control the explosion of alewife baitfish populations, they have secured a permanent home through natural reproduction and hatchery stockings. Due to the massive growth rates of both fish, which are vora-

Chinook salmon like this fall-run male display gorgeous
spawning colors.

cious feeders, chinook can reach 46 pounds and coho
up to 28 pounds. The tremendous sporting ability of
such large fish is well appreciated and sought after.
When one hooks a fresh-run king and experiences the
exhilarating leaps and runs of these fish, one will be a
fond admirer for life.

THE STEELHEAD/SALMON LIFECYCLE

Chinook salmon, as fall spawners, enter the rivers as early as July and early August on the St. Mary's River in northern Michigan and Ontario, and the cold spring-fed tributaries of Lake Michigan's Little Manistee and Pere Marquette systems. However, the majority of the run enters the rivers from late August through early November.

The coho can be an early fall runner, like on Michigan's St. Joseph or Wisconsin's Bois Brule, or a later runner—into late November—which is the case for the majority of Great Lakes salmon rivers. The smaller pink salmon (*Oncorhynchus gorbuscha*), averaging 2 to 4 pounds, was introduced to the Lake Superior tributaries in 1956 and is a popular gamefish that has bright colors and is found primarily in the Lakes Superior and Huron corridor.

Personalities and predispositions to take the fly vary among the Pacific salmon. When fresh into the river

An early-run coho shows why these fish are often called "silvers."

systems, schooled-up king, or chinook, salmon can be enticed to take a fly quite aggressively. However, they quickly go on the spawning urge, which greatly decreases their urge to strike.

Coho and pinks, on the other hand, tend to strike the fly much more eagerly and for a longer period of time. Coho, or "silvers," as they are known in Alaska, are compared to steelhead in their sporting behavior, with fish often being enticed to take a floating dry fly or brightly colored wets on a consistent basis.

Pacific salmon stocks are perhaps 90 to 100 percent wild on the Michigan tributaries to the lake that bears the state's name. Massive runs occur on the Pere Marquette, Muskegon, Manistee, and Platte systems, with wild runs that rival or surpass Alaska. Lakes Superior and Huron also have excellent wild and hatchery-reared Pacific salmon runs, along with New York's Salmon River on Lake Ontario. Pacific salmon can be distinguished from steelhead and Atlantic salmon by their dark mouths and gums, massive displays of teeth at full spawning development, and differently shaped tails and ventral fins.

ATLANTIC SALMON

Once indigenous to all Lake Ontario tributaries, *Salmo salar* were highly utilized by the Native Americans. When Europeans arrived in the New World, they decimated the runs to extinction by the late 1800s through over-harvesting and degradation of river ecosystems. With a continued effort by the New York

Atlantic salmon populations are being restored, and introduced, to Lakes Huron and Ontario.

Department of Environmental Conservation and Ontario Ministry of Fisheries, a several-decades-long program has begun to restore the historic runs that once occurred on New York's Salmon and Ontario's Credit Rivers. New York State has had the most luck producing good runs on its Salmon River and Oak Orchard Creek.

The showcase for Atlantics in the Great Lakes continues to be the St. Mary's River in Sault Ste. Marie Michigan/Ontario. The ice-cold, plankton-rich waters of Superior, which empties into Lake Huron's baitfish smorgasbord hunting grounds, provides the St. Mary's Atlantics with ideal North Atlantic ecosystem conditions. Lake Superior State, the pioneering aquatic laboratory that started the program back in the 1970s by importing Penobscot River– and Grand Lake–strain salmon from Maine, gets excellent and consistent runs of Atlantics up to 25 pounds. This fishery shows signs of only improving and has already achieved worldwide acclaim.

Atlantic salmon enter the rivers as early as late May and June and will run all summer until spawning in the late fall. Upon their first arrival they are chrome silver, opaque turquoise ghosts; near spawning, they adopt the beautiful orange and marbling colors of their close kin the brown trout (*Salmo trutta*) and are often mistaken for them.

As for its sporting possibilities on the fly, this fish needs no introduction, since countless books have been written about *salar*'s uncanny interest in all manner of fly presentations. Yet it makes a mockery out of the whole angling proposition due to its snobbish and indifferent personality at times—qualities that make this fish such a noble prize.

THE LIFE SUPPORT SYSTEM: THE MASSIVE FOOD CHAIN OF THE GREAT LAKES

Compared to a West Coast angler's fly box, the Great Lakes fly pattern assortment is impressionistic and highly detailed to cover the incredibly diverse food sources of the ecosystem. The food groups are broken into two categories: aquatic vertebrates and aquatic and terrestrial invertebrates.

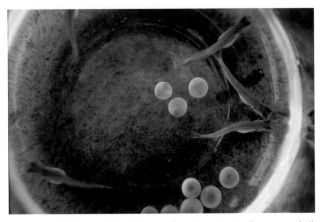

The perfect Glo-bug and hatching steelhead sac fry, the first stage of all salmonid life.

The aquatic vertebrates include the big-lake forage baitfish populations and riverine populations. Chinook salmon are notorious for being at the top of their food chain, with up to 90 percent of their diets composed of alewives. Other baitfish include smelt, bloater chubs, emerald shiners, shad, herring, stickle-back minnows, gobies, small perch, and walleye pike. In the river systems, sculpin, dace, sucker minnows, and steelhead and salmon fry are important forage.

Aquatic and terrestrial invertebrates are consumed in the lake and riverine feeding grounds. Plankton, *Mysis* and *Diporeia* shrimp, water boatmen, and aquatic insects such as mayflies and caddisflies are part of the lake forage. Terrestrial insects blown from lakeshore bluffs float on the "scum line" in the middle of the

The protein-rich biomass of the Great Lakes, such as alewives, emerald shiners, chubs, rainbow smelt, and herring, allow salmonids to grow fast and fat.

lakes, where steelhead surface feed on bees, beetles, and flying ants.

Riverine aquatic insect life, such as midges, small stoneflies, mayflies, and terrestrials is an important food source for salmonid fry and juveniles. However, drifting or emerging black stoneflies or *Hexagenia* mayflies will put adult steelhead and salmon in the river in a taking mood.

It is interesting to note that steelhead, coho, and Atlantic salmon will diversify their food intake 50/50 between the two groups. At times, steelhead consumption of invertebrates will be drastically higher—thus their incredible curiosity toward fly patterns.

Great Lakes rivers abound in insects like this cased caddis.

FROM THE GRAVEL WOMB TO THE BIG LAKE

Pacific and Atlantic salmonids of the Great Lakes have retained their evolutionary spawning processes and timetables with a great degree of accuracy, despite the harsh environmental factors they have encountered in their new homes. Their anadromous (salt water to fresh water) migration is now called potamadromous (fresh water to fresh water). The careful balancing of salinity in their bloodstreams is now not a necessary lifecycle complication. For this reason, along with the incredible forage-rich ecosystems of the Great Lakes and rivers, our salmonids have a larger window to feed or be persuaded to attack a fly once they've entered the riverine environment.

All Pacific salmonids (salmon and steelhead) and Atlantic salmon ascend their natal rivers from big lakes with a high degree of accuracy. Picking up the scent of their rivers of origin in an amazing three parts per million concentration is one of the most incredible olfactory marvels of nature. Each run is triggered by a genetic code of signals that detect appropriate photooptic periods of daylight in the migrating season and sexual reproductive gland development, and the ability to detect increases in river flows and proper migratory water temperatures. Once entering the river, the salmonid will spawn in as little as a month, or may go for six to twelve months in the river before spawning like steelhead and Atlantic salmon. It is, perhaps, this long duration of river residency that makes these fish restless, very inquisitive, and willing to take fly offerings.

When a female has secured spawning gravel, usually at a vast and well-oxygenated riffle or the tail-out of a pool, she will use her tail to dig a redd into the stream bottom. This redd, perhaps as deep as a foot, will protect the eggs and provide oxygen. A dominant male will move in, and the female squirts her eggs and he deposits his milt. Anywhere from three to six thousand eggs can be deposited depending on the size of the female. For Pacific and Atlantic salmon, which spawn in the fall and early winter, maturation time for the eggs can be from ninety to a hundred days, depending on water temperatures. The eggs will remain in the cold river waters through winter, hatching in late winter or early spring. Steelhead, which are late-winter and spring spawners, will have a shorter incubation time of thirty to sixty days, and their hatching will usually begin in May and June.

The first stage of emerging life is the alevin. It still has its attached yolk sac and hides in the gravel until the sac is absorbed; after which it is known as a fry. The fry then migrates towards the shoreline in search of tiny plankton, midges, scuds, and any aquatic invertebrate it can secure for nourishment. It next develops into a parr (characterized by barred markings along the side). A Pacific salmon will remain a parr for several months; steelhead and Atlantic salmon remain as parr for two to three years. Then on a mysterious night in the spring (late May through June), as the parr start to turn silver-sided, they will smolt en masse towards the big lake through a well-honed genetic signal that has been carried down in the species over the millennia. Their smolting migrations use the cloaking device of night, with an uncanny ability to pick a full moon and rivers swollen from recent rains. This is the ideal time to vanish to the big lake undetected and not preyed upon. Once in the big lake or ocean, the salmonids' sole purpose in life is to feed, gain weight, and return to their natal rivers as strong, dominant spawners.

The chief difference between Pacific salmon, steelhead, and Atlantic salmon is that the Pacific salmon will die after their first spawning, whereas the steelhead and Atlantics can spawn multiple times.

2

READING THE WATER AND
TIMING THE RUNS

Guide Dave Barber looks for that perfect pattern during a snow squall on New York's Salmon River.

The ultimate key to successful Great Lakes steelhead and salmon fly fishing lies in the angler's ability to understand and dissect the integral riverine components of structure and flow, along with comprehending how these elements shape and dictate the genetic predisposition of salmonids through the seasons. By combining natural environmental and man-induced factors that influence the run, the sweet secret to suc-

Reading the water for Skamania steelhead and Atlantic salmon.

cess can be methodically applied from one river to the next. Keep in mind, though, that it is still fishing—timing, patience, and good old dumb luck can still confound you despite your well-founded studies and methods.

Though salmon and steelhead are quite consistent in their migratory behavior, river systems change whimsically from year to year and from season to season. To say that fly fishing Lake Erie's "steelhead alley" is identical to fishing the tailwater and spring-fed rivers of Michigan is a gross misstatement. Though similar techniques apply, the waters are vastly different. One must read each river, species, and season as a separate

An angler prepares for a day of fun on a Great Lakes river.

case study to produce trophy salmonid on the fly in a consistent fashion.

For the most part, all Great Lakes rivers can be grouped into two categories. **Type I Rivers** consist of moderate gradients, subterranean spring flows, or tail-water releases, which form classic riffle/pocket/pool/tail-out river structure with numerous river bends. These waters are usually filled with ample spawning gravel and have somewhat stable and consistent flows. They are conducive to wild salmonid populations or are stocked heavily due to their appealing qualities for angling.

Type II Rivers are spate rivers of either high or low gradient, have great fluctuations in flow, and usually short sections of river for migration. Their characters can range from steep, austere shale/stone gradients to long, uneventful farmland/prairie structure with no river definition. Water tends to cool and ice over quickly, and also run rampant to flood stage levels during a warm spell. They also tend to run warm in the summer and silt with little to no natural reproduction. However, if good gravel and a sandy substrate exist along with spring-creek influences, natural reproduction can be significant, like on Lake Superior's steep gradient tributaries.

Does the type of river classification dictate how good the fishing will be? Absolutely not! Approximately 70 percent of our Great Lakes rivers maintain an aggressive salmonid stocking policy, which will dictate the numbers of returning fish. Type II waters often produce astounding angling over the more pris-

Steep-gradient rivers cut through rocky moraine, creating riffles, rapids, and pocket water.

tine and genetically safeguarded wild systems. A classic case in point is the highly productive and amazing fishery of Lake Erie's "steelhead alley," which extends from Ohio through Pennsylvania and into New York. Though for the most part these rivers are Type II, except for perhaps the Cattaraugus of New York, the millions of steelhead stocked here and the number of rivers in this sector provide phenomenal double-digit hook-ups when compared to the Type I wild waters of Michigan's Pere Marquette or Wisconsin's Bois Brule.

The glamour of absurd numbers of salmonid hook-ups has become the desirable yet self-destructing Trojan horse of the Great Lakes fishery. Excess breeds greed, which in turn shapes behaviors of disrespect for the fish and the resource. This eventually leads to a feeling of despair and emptiness when numbers of fish are no longer produced, as was the case on the Erie Tributary in the fall of 2003, after experiencing an ungodly number of steelhead the previous year—a quantity versus quality complex. One must always look at what is the desired total angling experience.

When dealing with Type I and II rivers, you have to focus on the variables that will produce the best success. Type II waters will be more succeptable to temperature and flow fluctuations than more stable Type I waters. Type I rivers are more consistent in flows and temperature—thus the timing of the trip can be made in the time honored "traditional peak periods." Type II waters must be approached individually and dealt with on a day-to-day basis of their flows and temperatures regardless of the traditional "right time to fish them."

Luckily, the Great Lakes fly angler of today has the luxury of choices. He or she may choose to fish wilderness rivers that run through national forests and support wild steelhead and salmon populations or nearby semiremote or urban fisheries that offer the same beautiful salmonids. The Great Lakes fishery, due to its close proximity to two-thirds of North America's population, must be maintained by a hatchery stocking program, along with preservation of wild populations where they can exist and prosper. The trend is to maintain stocking programs by using genetically unique wild strains of salmon and steelhead that have evolved over the past century in the Great Lakes system. We are, in essence,

Michigan guide Jeff Bacon preparing for action.

using a wild species whether it is caught in Cleveland or on a remote Lake Superior river.

DISSECTING THE RIVER

When rivers cut through rocky moraine substrate or experience elevation change, stream structure is formed. Combined with a river's path of flow, coupled with current deflection like river bends, channel structure, and obstructions, a river's character is displayed. A classic salmon/steelhead system will include the following—Section A: Riffles, rapids, and throat water; Section B: Pocket/boulder water; Section C: Pool, guts, and flats; Section D: The tail-out.

A magnificent chinook salmon busts water on Michigan's Muskegon River. Note the perfectly clear waters and spawning gravel, which produce over a million wild salmon each year through natural reproduction.

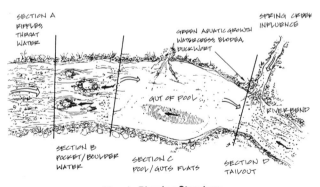

Classic Riverine Structure

In Sections A and B, the river cuts the rocky structure, thus creating the fast, nervous water with river structure of boulders stone and gravel. In Section C, the gradient is stabilized and deeper, and slower flows are maintained. Here, the gut, or drop-off trough, and flats are established that usually hold wooded structures. Finally, in Section D, the tail-outs spill over and are usually the start of another series of gradients. It is important to note that these sections can exist in short to long duration in river sections—anywhere from ten yards to as long as a mile. Environmental influences on rivers such as floods, droughts, shifting of the river channels, downed wooded debris, and spring creeks will tend to concentrate or spread out the salmonids in the river. Man-made dams or coffers will have a similar effect.

Throughout the year, environmental and genetic factors shape salmon and steelhead runs and their behavior. How they hold and migrate in the river system is

A beautiful winter-run female ready for release.

greatly affected by water temperatures, weather influence, river flows, barometric pressure and the most conducive time of day. Primary holding and moving lies will change depending on conditions. Rather than generalize, I will apply them to the various seasons and species the angler will encounter. However, some constant variables exist that can be applied to all salmonids during the four seasons.

Hydrodynamics—Going with the Flow

This is one of the most crucial factors that influences the upstream migration of salmon and steelhead. The need for migration is displayed in a fish's genetic predisposition to spawn. However, how a fish migrates

Atlantic salmon will go with the flow, using creases and seams for upstream migration.

depends on the complex interaction of the river's flow and temperature, coupled with the fish's stage of physiological development and metabolism.

An increase in river flow will be a strong signal for upstream migration. This remains consistent with all salmon and steelhead at all times of the year. During these increases, the migratory salmonids will negotiate the river system with a consistent and uncanny intuition.

CREASES AND SEAM TRANSITION WATER— HOLDING AND MOVING FISH AND THEIR TAKING LIES

Navigation with ease and conservation of metabolism are the fish's credos. By using the path of least resistance, many miles of river can be negotiated quickly by a salmon or steelhead. Creases and seams in the current exist where the faster and slower currents meet. These can often be found at the edge of a foam

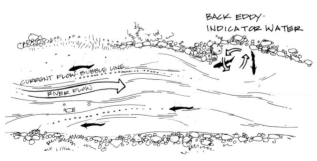

Seam/Crease Transition Water

The Douglaston water on New York's Salmon River.

GREAT LAKES SALMON AND STEELHEAD

or bubble line or where a back eddy meets the main flow. They are extremely important when coupled with emanating spring flows or the flow of creeks into the main river, especially during very cold or warm river conditions. These spring flows will be in the 48- to 56-degree range—the ideal temperatures preferred by steelhead and salmon—and draw fish in like a magnet. By using these flow demarcation lines, the fish can glide and slip in and out of the current, allowing them to conserve energy and maintain a steady upstream progress. Creases and seams are also created by flow deflections from boulder/pocket waters, river bends, woody debris like logjams, and in drops and contours of the river channel such as the gut of the pool. Moving fish will use shoreline areas, which have reduced flows, along with the crease and seam deflections created by the aforementioned structure.

Primary and Secondary Holding Lies

A large, wild female chinook with a precious cargo of eggs.

Holding fish will take up positions in lies that afford metabolic comfort, security, and hierarchical dominant positioning. The pool "gut," an area where there is a river bottom trough or drop-off, is an ideal holding area. The flats and tail-outs of the pool are slow flowing areas that are very soothing to moving fish that have begun to hold. Couple these areas with a logjam, a large boulder, or a shale shelf that will provide additional current defection and security, and you'll have the ultimate holding and taking lies.

The great debate exists between which fish is best to take a fly—a holder or a mover? Though a mover will take a fly if it is presented properly with the right timing to intercept the moving fish, a holding fish in its perfect realm is poised to inspect and be aroused by a

This fall-run steelhead crushed a pink Marabou Spey in a deep tail-out run.

The author with a perfect St. Mary's Atlantic salmon.

fly offering and is fixed on the river's flow and biological drift. A holding fish is much more aware of its surrounding environment, and a moving fish is preoccupied with traveling as quickly as it can. Though water temperatures greatly affect upstream migration, they are extremely seasonal.

BAROMETRIC PRESSURE AND TIME OF DAY

Through the millennia, ocean-going salmonids have learned to adjust their highly sensitive air bladders to sea-level depths and shallow river dwellings. It makes sense that barometric pressure, which is an air and water compressing action, plays on their bladder. One can deduce that a rapidly falling barometer usually signals a frontal system of inclement weather and possible precipitation. These would be ideal conditions for migration and would curtail the bite. On the flip side, a rising or stable high barometric reading would signal stable weather and sunny skies, which would promote holding and conditions for fish to go on the grab. Holding fish tend to become quite anxious or bored, and thus display hunt-and-play behavioral responses. Steelhead and salmon will take the fly well at consistently low or high pressure—the key being the word "consistent." Drastic fluctuations bring changes in behavior.

As for the time of day when angling is best, this varies considerably. Since salmon and steelhead are

Tatsuya Kamoshita gets an early start in the search for Atlantic salmon on the St. Mary's River.

READING THE WATER AND TIMING THE RUNS 37

very optic sensitive and prefer low-light levels, dawn's first light and dusk's last glimmer have always been productive times. These times can also correlate to the salmonids' instinctive predatory behavior in the big lake, as they are conducive to capturing schools of baitfish and shrimp.

Salmon and steelhead upriver migrations usually take place from the early evening through the night and into early dawn. This is the reason for the first-light fishing advantage: You may be fishing to freshly migrated schools of fish that just came in and have taken up a holding position as daylight approaches. Migration is also in full swing during inclement weather such as heavy rain, thunder, and snow storms,

A chrome chinook salmon taken in August just as it entered a Great Lakes river.

which create low-light conditions and distort the river's surface window. Full-moon cycles are also very conducive to nighttime salmonid migrations.

Pacific and Atlantic salmon tend to migrate in large schools. Steelhead, however, tend to be more nomadic in their migration; favoring small groups or singular journeys, particularly winter fish. Exceptions exist with summer steelhead and smaller tribu-

The author admires an inland Atlantic salmon. These fish can now be found from New York's Finger Lakes to northern Michigan.

tary steelhead migrations, which must wait for ideal river flows and temperatures before ascending the river. When they finally get the right signal, it might be a stampede.

THE GREAT LAKES SEASONS – TIMING THE RUNS

The old adage that timing is everything cannot hold truer than with salmon and steelhead runs. The traditional peak periods have progressively vanished due to major fluctuations in weather patterns, giving us warm or extremely cold seasons coupled with droughts and floods. To the salmon/steelhead fly fisher or outfitter trying to plan and time the runs, it has been maddening. However, thanks to the Internet and the increasingly hospitality-oriented nature of reputable guides and outfitters, your chances for a successful outing have greatly improved.

On the Internet, Great Lakes surface water temperatures can be accessed at www.coastwatch.msu.edu. These are especially helpful in predicting when steelhead and salmon upstream migrations and surf-fishing opportunities will occur, particularly during very warm summer and early fall periods. When river-mouth temperatures drop from the 70-degree range into the 50s due to offshore winds, runs of summer steelhead and early fall Pacific salmon will occur. Also, after brutally cold winters, the warming up of the shore's waters will trigger the spring spawning migration of steelhead.

To monitor river flows and temperatures, visit the U.S. Geological Survey site at www.USGS.gov for accurate and current river flow and temperature status so you don't show up at rivers that are blown out or dry. Also, www.weather.com can help detect frontal systems, barometric pressure, and wind directions.

It is also wise and good long-term planning to establish a relationship with a reputable guide or outfitter who will give you credible reports, along with helpful advice. These operators are looking to make a long-term, devoted client out of you, as well.

In addition, several report/chat-room sites exist, such as www.steelheadsite.com and www.flyfisherman.com, which can provide information. However, the problem with these sites is that they are anonymous, so their credibility is often severely lacking. Remember, "garbage in, garbage out," so critique your leads with discretion.

Finally, despite the great cyber information and what "Joe the guide" told you, you have to be on the water through the prime runs to catch a fish. With conditions changing very quickly in the Great Lakes, today's news could already be last week's news. I can't tell you how many times my clients and I have had great steelhead and salmon fishing when the Internet and everyone else said the run wasn't on yet, or that it was over and the fishing was no good. Once again, these are the humbling factors that make salmonid fishing so simple and yet so perplexing—

Chinook and coho salmon usually hit Michigan's famous Pere Marquette River when the autumn colors appear.

this is what makes it fun and keeps bringing you back for more.

AUTUMN

Fall brings a plethora of salmonid fly-fishing opportunities. Pacific salmon such as chinook, coho, and pinks will be in their prime spawning runs. Winter steelhead strains will enter the river system on the heels of the salmon or as the rivers cool down, and Atlantic salmon and lake-run browns will be sporting their beautiful mocha-orange marbled spawning colors and exaggerated kypes.

The Pacific salmon will begin staging in the lakes around August. Very early runs of chinook exist in Michigan's ice-cold, spring-fed tributaries, such as the Little Manistee and Pere Marquette. The St. Mary's River, located between Lakes Superior and Huron, also has spawning chinooks in July. As the daylight photoperiod diminishes, the chinook, coho, and pink salmon become sexually mature. If the rivers are very low or warm, good surf-fishing opportunities will exist.

When cold-weather frontal systems push in, bringing storms with ample rains, massive upstream migrations will occur as river levels rise and cool. This is the initial spawning phase. Once they arrive in the rivers, the

Note the pink bars on this large "pinook," a cross between a chinook and a pink salmon on the St. Mary's.

READING THE WATER AND TIMING THE RUNS   **43**

schools will choose large, deep pools to hold in until they are sexually mature—which can happen anytime from a week to several months. This is the phase where they are notorious for jumping, splashing, and rolling on the surface. At this stage, they are very aggressive and will attack a swinging fly or streamer. Keep in mind that the fish are suspended in the pool from the surface to the bottom, so vary your depths of presentation. A sinking-tip line or running/shooting line with some weight to get the flies down is swung in a down-and-across fashion through the pools. The strikes will be either subtle or rod jarring.

Once the salmon move to gravel spawning beds, they can be very difficult to induce to strike your fly. In rivers with natural reproduction, smaller nymphs usu-

This salmon fell to a Glo-bug.

ally seem to trigger memories of the juvenile feeding habits. Strikes will usually result from the aggressive response to intrusion into the spawning redds. Streamers, Spey flies, and large nymphs are the key. The Boss, Comet, Egg-Sucking Leech, Picasse Spey, and sculpin-style patterns produce well. The angler can either use the strike indicator/nymph method or down-and-across swing on a one- or two-handed rod. The bottom-bounce nymphing method using the running/ shooting presentation (chuck-and-duck) is also very popular. Keep in mind that during this languid phase of the spawning run, the salmon will need repeated presentations to entice them to strike. When females are releasing eggs in good numbers, dominant and subordinate salmon, steelhead, lake-run browns, and resident trout will partake of this feeding frenzy. Watching the color and size of your egg pattern is critical.

Perhaps the ultimate sporting experience for the fly fisher lies in fall steelheading. This is the time of year when Great Lakes anglers can present their flies in the West Coast traditional down-and-across swing method. River water temperatures are usually ideal, and the steelhead still have the search-and-destroy feeding instinct. Their chrome color, leaping and fighting ability, and willingness to take a variety of fly presentations puts them at the pinnacle of the Great Lakes experience.

Fall steelhead are winter-strain fish that spawn in the late winter and spring. Fall-run fish may be late returning summer-strain steelhead. Fall runs of steelhead can be significant one year and minimal the next year. The

This healthy fall-run chrome steelhead crushed an orange weave egg pattern.

following factors are critical in triggering fall steelhead runs. The **Window of Opportunity** is perhaps the most important phase. Here river temperatures align with near-shore lake temperatures and provide a major carpet ride of upstream migration. If water levels and flows are at normal or above stages, this will further enhance the run. However, steelhead will choose temperature over flow as the most significant factor. The **Genetic Code** of strains of winter steelhead is also important since some strains, like the Chamber's Creek and Little Manistee strains, are significant fall runners. **Pheromone Attraction**, the strong sexual spawning scent given off by salmon and brown trout, is another key element that will induce the run.

The fall run of winter steelhead takes place in phases. In the initial migration phase, the fish's metabolism is in overdrive, and it will strike a swinging Spey fly or streamer, or a dead-drifted nymph or egg pattern, with a vengeance. If significant spawning of salmon and brown trout is taking place, they will mosey right up to the edges of the spawning redds and

A happy angler with a steelhead that attacked a hot orange and pink Marabou Spey.

appear as turquoise/gray ghosts, darting nervously away from the huge teeth of kype-jawed and aggressive salmon. Here, they are looking for an easy meal of eggs.

As long as river temperatures remain ideal (40 to 54 degrees F), the steelhead will take up primary river lies and strike the fly with uncanny accuracy and consistency. The angler should experiment with various colored Spey flies, baitfish streamer imitations, and egg patterns. Fall steelhead are fond of pool tail-outs and guts of the pool, especially when combined with

Mark Danhausen ready to release a fall steelhead back to a Michigan stream.

wooded debris as shelter and river bends. Boulders and shale/rock ledges also provide ideal holding lies. Fall steelhead, due to their shallow-water disposition, have been known to take a skating or waking dry fly, especially in the shallow tail-outs. This technique has been most productive on the shallower river tributaries of Lake Erie, especially when they are crammed full of steelhead during a warm fall with low water levels. The sheer competition for primary holding space will trigger the aggressive response levels necessary for surface enticement.

Atlantic salmon and lake-run browns, which look very similar during their fall spawning periods, are a lot more skittish than their Pacific salmon counterparts. They traditionally are late spawners (late October

Fishing baitfish imitations on a sink-tip line can be very effective for aggressive lake-run browns.

through December). Atlantics are very responsive to swinging baitfish imitations such as sculpins, emerald shiners, and Muddlers. Lake-run browns are more gullible and can flip the switch from skittish to gluttonous at a moment's notice. The browns tend to favor streamers like Woolly Buggers, Egg-Sucking Leeches, sculpins, dull baitfish patterns, and washed-out egg-pattern colors that range from duller peach/cream to the rotting and decaying unfertilized egg color of bluish purple. The blue color phenomenon, par-

Mike Froy with a big chinook buck that inhaled a black leech pattern right at dusk.

ticularly strong in Lakes Erie and Ontario, could possibly be due to the extreme abundance of unfertilized eggs from the less successful spawning endeavors of hatchery-raised salmonids.

WINTER STEELHEADING

Each year, as I think I'm growing wiser, I try to put some reason to the method and madness of this angling-cult phenomenon. The Great Lakes region has swelled the ranks and obsession of winter steelheaders. Bone-chilling sub-zero wind chills, white-out lake-effect snow squalls, and rivers filled with ice and slush will not quell the enthusiasm of the winter steelhead junkie. You only need to go to New York's Salmon River when 30 inches of snow has piled up overnight and see the anglers' parking lots filled to capacity. Or visit a Michigan river and see guide drift boats cut through shelf ice to get a line wet. This is steelhead passion in full force. It all boils down to this fish, which through the millennia has evolved to become the only full-fledged game specimen to migrate and hold in ice-cold rivers. It will strike the fly and provide valiant sport when other piscatorial predators lie dormant.

Winter steelheading is worth the pursuit since up to 60 percent of the spring spawning run is already residing in the pools and runs of the Great Lakes tributaries. Throughout the winter, especially during spate periods from warm-spell thaws, steelhead will migrate up the rivers. Once in the system, they will lower their me-

This monstrous winter-run buck displays a pronounced "kype."

tabolism and hold in the most comfortable parts of the rivers. Target your angling efforts around pool guts and flats, outside seams of river bends, and especially where warmer spring seeps and creeks come into the main river.

Flies must be presented so they dead-drift near the bottom where the fish are. The bottom strata presents the least current flow. Utilize techniques such as bottom nymphing with the chuck-and-duck sliding weights system (e.g., slinkie, pencil lead) and strike indicator presentations. Keep the speed of the drift slower than the current.

Though most winter fish are lethargic due to their lowered metabolism (except for freshly migrated newcomers), they still possess a strong curiosity for fly presentations. Several factors heighten the interest and fly-taking potential for holding winter fish. A slight 1- to 2-degree rise in water temperature, perhaps on a sunny day, may turn on the bite. The biological stream drift of hatching midges or stoneflies can play a pronounced influence. Territorial jockeying for hierarchical dominance will also arouse the competitive sexual-aggressive behavior of the males and females that will soon spawn.

Fly patterns should revolve around biological drift components like stonefly, *Hexagenia,* and caddis when some insect movement is detected. Egg and Estaz colors should capture the changing spawning colors of the fish with pinks, cerise, and flame-orange tones. To newly migrated chrome fish, chartreuse and electric blue have a particular appeal, especially in murkier spate flows. Finally, resident baitfish streamer imitations will often provoke the territorial aggressive behavior. Focus on sculpins, shiners, dace, and small salmon-parr imitations.

Time your fishing around the most comfortable and warmest time of the day—afternoons to dusk. A steady, high barometric pressure is often desired during winter periods; avoid a marked drop in pressure, which signals a frontal system. The winter bite just before dark is usually the best, especially in low, clear waters. Also, the dusk period will arouse holding dominant fish to cruise their primary areas or prepare for a nocturnal migration.

Persistence, patience, and tough mental visioning that each cast may produce a fish are necessary. Each primary holding lie must be worked thoroughly from top to bottom and at different times of the day. Remember, you are trying to provoke a sleeping giant to strike your fly. Strike detection can be subtle or rod jolting. Focus on watching your rod tip to see the head-shaking, bouncing motion that is not immediately detected by feel but signals a strike.

Also, complete each drift fully, allowing for a little hang time at the end. Winter fish will often slowly follow your offering until it stops swinging. Strikes can often be very subtle—strike at every sudden pause. Self-discipline and a lot of optimism is the key to winter steelheading.

Laurie Supinski casts to fresh late-spring steelhead. Spring steelheading has become an upper Great Lakes tradition.

THE SPRING RUN

As the photoperiod of daylight increases and water temperatures warm, the sexual maturation of the steelhead is approaching the ripe phase for mating. The hunt for spawning gravel is on, as holdover and brand new lake-run arrivals converge on the tail-outs and

Dr. John Murphy with a brightly colored buck steelhead that inhaled a Steelhead Hammer nymph.

throat riffle waters where egg-laying redds will be dug. Fishing to spawning salmonids is a common practice in the Great Lakes. However, one may choose not to do so if he or she decides it unethical. Wild steelhead populations are more affected than hatchery-reared populations. When fishing gravel spawning beds, do it in a sporting fashion by avoiding foul hooking fish. Hook setting should be done when a fish is visibly shaking its head from a strike, rather than from the angler's reaction to the fish's body movements. Often, their quick, jittery movements are the result of trying to get away from a fly as opposed to being drawn to it.

Spring steelheading has three distinct phases. For fresh-run spring fish, target the pool's gut, flats, and tail-outs and any dark holding water below or above spawning gravel. These fish are often not ready to spawn, but are very eager to strike a fly. Pattern selection for gravel areas usually revolves around biological drift insects dislodged during the redd digging by females and stray unfertilized washed-out eggs. Caddis larvae, stonefly, small *Hexagenia,* and scud nymph imitations work well. General attractor patterns like the Hare's Ear, Prince, soft hackles, and Copper Johns also produce. A swinging Egg-Sucking Leech or Picasse Spey will often aggravate a large alpha-back male to slam the fly.

In the gravel phase, the angler is fishing blind, dead-drifting nymph or egg patterns or swinging small wets and streamers on or near the botton to the actual redds or in the drop-off pockets below and above. Fly

Fresh spring steelhead have a distinctive reddish cheek.

patterns should consist of chartreuse and bright fluorescent egg and Estaz patterns, attractor Speys, and baitfish streamer imitations. The steelhead Woolly Bugger is a hot pattern for these fish. As the angler is drifting these flies through the gravel areas, he should focus on the line entering the water. Any quick, sudden stops by the line can be a strike or a snag. If it starts to move, it's a fish on!

Finally, in the drop-back phase, post-spawn steelhead will stage their migration down to the big lake. Once having spawned, they have a ravenous appetite and are eager to put on body weight. If good food sources exist in the river system, like insects, newly hatched salmon fry, sucker spawn, and sculpin/dace baitfish, present fly patterns. Target areas where the most abundant food

The author and his son, Peter, pose with a drop-back hen steelhead that hammered a chinook fry streamer.

source can be found, such as shoreline areas for salmon baitfish, behind sucker redds, and in pocket water for hatching insects.

THE SUMMER FISHERY

Perhaps one of the most exciting and under-explored aspects of Great Lakes salmonids is the emerging opportunity for summer steelhead and Atlantic salmon. The summer Skamania steelhead is found mainly in Lake Michigan and Lake Ontario tributaries. The Atlantic salmon runs exist in fishable numbers on Michigan/Ontario's St. Mary's River and New York's Salmon River and Oak Orchard Creek. Smaller popu-

This massively girthed St. Mary's Atlantic salmon was binging on a school of rainbow smelt in late June.

lations can be found on the north shore of Lake Superior and on Ontario's Credit River. New York State and the province of Ontario are committed to the restoration of this once indigenous species to Lake Ontario.

Both fish are magnificent leapers and fighters when hooked and display the chrome-silver, fresh-run colors. Their upstream migration can occur anytime from mid-May through September, with the peak being June through August.

Certain conditions must be necessary for runs of summer steelhead and Atlantic salmon. They are genetically programmed to run during the long photo daylight periods of summer when rivers often run warm and low. Primarily, a strong offshore wind, which blows warm beach water out into the lake and brings in an undertow of cold water, is necessary to inaugurate the runs. If it is matched with a strong cold front of inclement storm and rains to raise river levels, significant migrations will take place. The best runs of both fish usually occur during cooler and wetter summers.

If offshore winds drive river-mouth beach temperatures from the normal high 70s down to the cooler 50s, but river temps run warm and water levels low, schools of summer steelhead and Atlantics will congregate off the river-mouth piers. This is when surf casting for these chromers is successful by double-hauling or overhead Spey casting sinking-tip lines with lake baitfish streamers like alewife and rainbow-

The St. Joseph River in Michigan hosts a nice run of Skamania-strain summer steelhead.

smelt patterns. Also, fluorescent Bunny Leeches and Marabou Speys in chartreuse, electric blue, hot pink, and orange are very effective for surf or freshly migrated fish.

Once the river migration takes place, summer steelhead and Atlantic salmon will run in schools. The Skamania steelhead will run the river system quickly, since

Walt Zimmerman and the author with a summer steelhead that smoked a black and purple leech pattern.

Fran Verdoliva, New York's Salmon River coordinator and a former guide, swings his favorite Muddler imitation for summer steelhead and Atlantic salmon.

they were genetically bred to do so. Atlantics will stage and be more pragmatic with their upstream migration.

Locating summer steelhead and Atlantics in the river is a function of locating oxygenated water and cold spring-creek seepages into the main river. Fast boulder/pocket throat water is an excellent place to start probing. Atlantics, with their anchoring pectoral fins, can hold in the fastest water. Steelhead will use the crease/seam cushion water provided by boulders. Pools and deep, fast tail-outs will also concentrate fish, especially in low water flows. When cold spring-creek influences are located, target the shoreline and holding water immediately downstream from the source.

Summer steelhead and Atlantic salmon in river holding lies will maintain an aggressive disposition to strike the fly as long as water temperatures remain below the 70-degree mark; water temperatures above this will stress the fish and make them languid. Significant drops in barometric pressure on cold frontal systems with storms and rain will often change the dull demeanor of the fish back to being on the bite.

Both summer steelhead and Atlantics love a swinging fly presentation. Steelhead, with their slower attack speeds, will also target dead-drift nymph presentations. Atlantics are fond of surface or near-surface imitations. As for color preferences in fly patterns, summer steelhead favor electric blue/purple and black imitations

The author's Leechsicle and Tasmanian Sculpin rabbit-strip patterns are great choices for steelhead and Atlantics.

along with fluorescent-yellow/chartreuse designs. Atlantics prefer the Muddler/sculpin motifs coupled with yellow/gold tones, especially on New York's Salmon River. Bomber-style dries will also elicit strikes.

On the large, open-water river system of the St. Mary's, Atlantics show a strong penchant for feeding on schools of rainbow smelt. They also show a curiosity for emerging caddis and *Hexagenia* mayflies and feed aggressively on *Mysis* shrimp, which are native freshwater crustaceans that populate the Great Lakes in significant numbers, particularly in plankton-rich environments. They provide an extremely rich food source for young and adult salmonids. Swinging Speys and Bombers in the upper rapids is also productive.

3

GREAT LAKES TACKLE AND ACCESSORIES

In general, steelhead and salmon tackle and gear used around the world can be applied to the Great Lakes. With greatly advanced technology, especially in the field of reels, rods, and lines, tackle has become refined to meet specific angling situations.

RODS

Without question, this is the most important equipment decision a steelhead/salmon fly angler will make. Rods fall into two specific categories: single-handed and two-handed Spey or Spey-style rods. Single-handed rod weights are geared towards targeted species. For steelhead, smaller Atlantics, lake-run browns, and smaller Pacific salmon like coho and pinks, a 6- to 8-weight rod is preferred in the 9- to 11-foot range. Some manufacturers are even making ultra-light 10-foot, 5-weights for steelhead.

On big rivers, you'll need a rod with a mid-flex taper along with a good fighting butt. The extra length provides greater mending and drift control on long casts, lifts more line off the water during nymphing, provides greater strike detection, and offers better tippet protection. It should also be lightweight (5 ounces) to allow for high-stick holding all day. The fighting butt should be large enough to accommodate fingerless

A large-arbor reel helped Laurie Supinski land this powerful Atlantic salmon.

gloves during cold weather. These rods are modeled after the Great Lakes "noodle" spinning rods, which were built to fish very light tippets that detect subtle strikes, particularly in winter. As for chinook salmon and Atlantics over 20 pounds, a 9- or 10-weight tip-flex with a strong butt section is needed to tame salmon up to 40 pounds.

Two-handed Spey rods come in three actions: European, traditional, and overhead styles. The European taper is a fast-action, butt-section-loading rod for a quicker casting style and the underhand cast. The traditional is a softer, more limber rod that loads throughout its length and accommodates slower casting styles and will execute all the various Spey casts: single, double, snap-t, single roll, etc. The overhead rod still uses two hands, but is very stiff and capable of throwing shooting heads at great distances without the water-loading anchor of a Spey cast. Some light 11½- to 12½-foot Euro-Speys are ideal single-handed nymphing rods due to their light 4- to 5-ounce weights and extremely sensitive tips for strike detection.

The tapers should accommodate your casting style and how you were taught. On smaller streams and rivers, the 12½-foot lengths are ideal. Bigger waters require greater line-lifting power—hence the 14- and 15-foot length.

REELS

Unlike trout and smaller gamefish fly fishing, where most often the fish are stripped in and the reel is

Shawn Murphy shows off a large male steelhead that tested her drag system to the limit.

mostly used as a line storage unit, the reel for steelhead and salmon is extremely important in that it functions to fight fish. Due to the uncanny ability of salmon or steelhead to produce hard-driving or charging runs and tremendous leaps at breathtaking speeds, the angler must immediately get the excess line on the reel and fight the fish off the reel's drag system. Stripping and fumbling with the line has no place in this type of combat.

Large-arbor reels are a must. They can pick up triple the amount of line in one reel versus conventional models. Their drag surfaces are up to 45 percent larger, minimizing torque on drag start-up and preventing break-offs. They are also being built extremely lightweight, with greater widths for more line storage. Reel handles should be large enough for quick reeling, but not too obtrusive, which can get in the way and break off a fish. Anti-reverse models are very beneficial to novices and prevent knuckle busters, where a fast-spinning handle slams into your fingers.

In the Great Lakes, it is important to make sure the drag system is sealed so that moisture is not allowed in to freeze up your reel, especially during winter steelheading. Also, make sure the fit between the spool and frame is very tight and not wobbly. Since Great Lakes nymphing often requires chuck-and-duck, thin-diameter running/shooting lines, they can get caught or pop out of loose spools.

Finally, make sure the drag system is smooth, with a low start-up inertia. Also, an interchangeable extra spool at an affordable price is a must. The bottom line is that there is a large arbor reel to fit everyone's price range and style preference.

LINES, LEADERS, AND TIPPETS

A diversity of fly lines is required to execute all the necessary presentations to Great Lakes salmon and steelhead. Since we are dealing with a fusion of salmonid species and extremes in river flows, depths, and methods of fly presentation, the New Age technological line specialist will have fun. However, simplicity is my purpose here, and I will present the basic lines with some unique specialty lines. The bottom-drift-nymphing method (a.k.a chuck-and-duck) is the universal workhorse technique for deep fly presentations with drag-free drifts when salmonids are on the bottom and not willing to budge too far to take the fly. This technique is extremely effective for cold water conditions or on gravel spawning areas. Running/shooting lines are thin and have a diameter between .027 and .034 inch. They are usually braided Dacron or mono cores with a slick fly-line coating. They are intermediate lines designed to be used with lead—either slinkies, spilt shot, or pencil varieties. They come in various colors of lime, orange, or clear mono. These lines load up the rod through the lead's ability to shoot the line. These running/shooting intermediate sinking lines are available from all the top-line companies.

If casting lead is not for you, sinking-tip, full-sinking and intermediate-sinking lines will get your flies down. Density-compensated sinking lines sink tip first, allowing for a straight profile between you and the fly. Sink rates vary from 1 to 7 inches per second and come in a class system (II being the slowest sinking, VI being fastest) and grains (200, 600—200 is the lightest). Super-fast sinking-tip lines have a 5- to 15-foot sinking tip on a weight-forward floating line, and are ideal for swinging a fly. Also, several manufacturers produce poly-leader sink tips that can be loop connected to your fly line.

Floating lines are used for swinging Spey-style wet flies, nymphing in shallow streams with or without lead, and for using strike-indicator methods. A weight-forward design is usually adequate. However, the new

This male Atlantic salmon took a smelt streamer on a full-sinking line.

salmon/steelhead taper, offered by all the boutique line companies, is the way to go. It incorporates a longer belly and fine back taper to allow for greater efficiency in line mending, roll casting, and single-handed Spey casting. They are also used to create greater casting distances on big rivers under windy and inclement weather conditions. Couple this with the new slick coating technology, which reduces friction and has greater floatability from the increased density of micro balloons in the line's coating layer, and you have the ultimate line.

Two-handed Spey tapers vary from line heads that are shorter (54 feet long) to ones that are larger (82 feet). The shorter heads are better for the popular 12½-foot-long European Spey rods. Most Spey lines average around 60 to 65 feet long in the head, allowing the Spey angler to master all the basic casts. Spey lines come with interchangeable tips, which include clear intermediate to various sinking tips.

Leaders and tippets vary and are dictated by presentation, fishing conditions, and the size of salmonids to be encountered. In chuck-and-duck drift nymphing, usually size 0X tippet material is Nail-Knotted to the running line and extended for 8 to 14 feet (depending on depth of the river) to the swivel. From the swivel, 1X to 5X tippets are used depending on the size of the fish, the size of flies, and water clarity. Manufactured salmon/steelhead–specific leaders have thick butt sections and quick tapers to drift flies naturally and take abrasions from violent strikes.

For basic indicator nymphing, the following leader formula usually holds consistent: First 30 inches—.020-inch diameter; next 27 inches—.017; 21 inches—.015; 12 inches—.011. Run your 2X to 4X tippet to the flies, and place split shot as needed.

As for leader and tippet material preference, there are two schools of thought. The old tried-and-true traditional Maxima-style mono, with its stiffness and abrasion resistance, has been the standard. However, thanks to the improving technology, fluorocarbon offers an invisible refractory index and a specific gravity of 1.76, which breaks through the surface tension quickly. Fluorocarbon has become the mainstay material for salmon and steelhead.

Indicator nymphing with a floating line is a productive steelheading technique. This late-spring fish was taken on Michigan's Muskegon River.

The new fluorocarbons have become extremely abrasion resistant, have improved knot strength, and have become more affordable. Since most Great Lakes steelhead and salmon are caught in rocky, boulder-strewn rivers with wooded debris, abrasion has always been a concern. Also, since fishing pressure has increased and waters clear rapidly throughout the entire Great Lakes system due to the exotic zebra mussel invaders, a stealth material is needed. Paramount to the new fluorocarbon generation is the added pound test strength. Where the old 2X (.009 inch) diameter materials tested at 8 pounds, they are now pushing the 12-pound test hold limits.

As for knots, we'll keep them simple. For fly line to backing, and leader to fly line, an Albright or Nail Knot is used, as well as a Triple Surgeon's or Blood Knot, the Surgeon's being stronger. As for attaching the tippet to the fly, the Trilene Knot is the strongest knot possible. The Duncan Loop, or Uni-Knot, is also effective. The Improved Turle Knot is useful for swinging wet flies with up- or downturned hook eyes.

Other incidentals in the rigging area include weights, swivels, beads, and strike indicators. In chuck-and-duck bottom drifting, the weight is secured well above the flies to allow for a long drag-free drift. When fishing pools or deep runs, a slip weight is usually attached to a snap or barrel swivel. This will swing up and down the main (0X) leader section. It can be in the form of parachute-cord "slinkies," pencil lead, or crimped split shot on a mono dropper. A small ceramic bead should

The Duncan Loop (Uni-Knot)

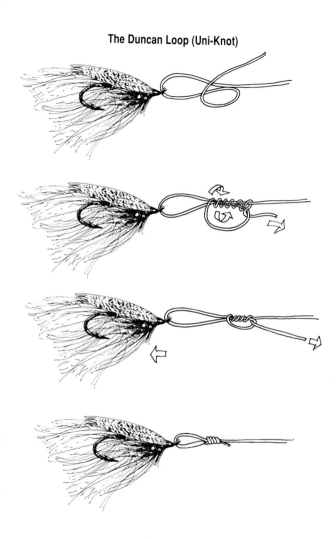

Improved Turle Knot

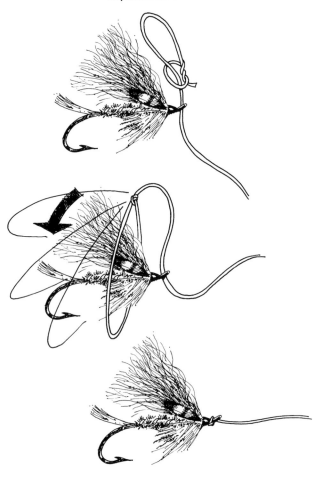

This perfect female steelhead ate a Golden Orange Nuke Egg.

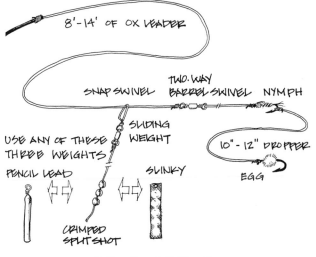

8' - 14' OF OX LEADER

SNAP SWIVEL

TWO-WAY BARREL SWIVEL   NYMPH

SLIDING WEIGHT

USE ANY OF THESE THREE WEIGHTS

PENCIL LEAD

SLINKY

10" - 12" DROPPER

EGG

CRIMPED SPLIT SHOT

Bottom Nymph Drifting Rig

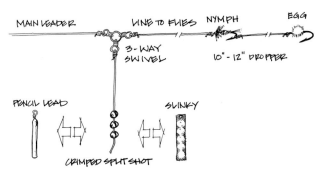

MAIN LEADER   LINE TO FLIES   NYMPH   EGG

3-WAY
SWIVEL   10" - 12" DROPPER

PENCIL LEAD   SLINKY

CRIMPED SPLIT SHOT

Tightline Rig for Runs and Pockets

be placed between the weight and the barrel swivel that joins the flies. The beauty of this rig is that salmonids will pick up the free-drifting nymph or egg patterns and not feel the weight tugging. This will often allow them to hold on to the fly longer for a better hook-set.

When fishing tight pocket water on shallower gravel, a three-way swivel rig will get the flies down quickly and allow for sharper strike detection: one eye goes to the leader, one has a dropper of weight, and the other eye goes to the flies. Since lead is not environmentally friendly, several manufacturers are making weight out of tin or tungsten.

WADERS AND DRESSING FOR THE ELEMENTS

With the extreme weather conditions the Great Lakes fly angler is subjected to, this category is just as important as the fly, rod, and reel. Waders should be of the boot-foot model to allow warm air to circulate and keep feet toasty. Many boot foots are lined with Thinsulate®, and when coupled with a thick wool and underlined moisture-wicking sock, you'll be able to tolerate icy flowing waters. Neoprene chest waders should be in the 3 to 5 mm varieties. In warmer weather, the various "no sweat" breathable waders are preferred. Wading pants and under-layering should be of Polar Fleece/Polartec® material with a thin underlayer of silk weight Capilene® to wick moisture away from the skin.

As for the rest of the body, silk-weight Capilene is the skin layer base, followed by various layers of Polar Fleece/Polartec® and combination wicking, insulation and wind-block systems like Regulator® and Orvis's Storm Chaser vest and Gale Force pullover systems. The final layer is the hooded waterproof and breathable storm jacket—perhaps the most expensive part of clothing. Make sure these nylon jackets are treated with a 100 percent waterproof finish, have large chest and back storage pockets for fly boxes and gear, cuff gussets with Velcro, stretch cuffs to seal out water, and hood and waist drawstrings.

To keep your head toasty, a Polartec® or wool/fur hat with a brim to keep snow or rain off your polarized glasses is a must. The head is the body's thermostat—it needs to stay covered. Gloves should be the fingertip-exposed models that have Velcro flaps to cover the exposed fingers when not in use. The best ones are constructed out of windproof micro fleece with a suregrip palm material. Larger nylon/Gore-Tex® outershell gloves can be used to keep the fleece gloves dry.

Communication between guide and client is essential for a great outing.

In extreme cold, hand-warmer heat packets are inserted to keep hands warm. In very cold conditions, take periodic breaks to warm your hands and toes. Build a fire by the river where allowed, or carry a small propane heater. Hot beverages or a nip of cognac can save the day. Don't overdo the alcohol—it will shrink your blood vessels and make you colder over time. Keep well hydrated by drinking lots of water.

When wading, use a staff and boot cleats. Adjustable-strap cleats, with either a hard rubber or steel frame, are suggested. New replaceable tungsten spikes are the way to go. Always wade cold rivers with a fellow angler or with others nearby. A CO_2 floatation cartridge vest is also highly advised. Paramount to wading cold Great Lakes rivers is your ability to read the river bottom and know the current flow, which is available from fishing reports or on the USGS Web site.

INCIDENTALS AND SOUND ADVICE

Gadgets have made salmon/steelhead fishing much easier and can increase your effectiveness. The following list should be considered as essential, along with some words of wisdom from your author/guide.

- Thermometer for testing water temperatures.
- Wristwatch with barometer and a wake-up alarm.
- Ice-off paste.
- Multi-tool (Leatherman® variety).
- Pliers/forceps to avoid sharp salmonid teeth.
- Catch-and-release mesh landing net with magnet coiled lanyard.

- Hook-sharpening stone.
- Nail-Knot tool.
- Strike indicators: poly/yarn or balsa adjustable types.
- Dry bags with extra clothes in case you take a plunge.
- 100-percent polarized sunglasses—the new Luminator® models adjust to various light levels.
- Detailed topographic and other maps of the area you fish.
- Seek out the services of reputable guides and outfitters to better educate you on the rivers you fish.

A Boga-grip allows you to photograph, weigh, and properly revive your fish with minimal handling.

- Don't plan your success based on the calendar. Use sound data like water temperatures, flows, and the knowledge of outfitters.
- Fish-grip glove for photographs. A fish filleting glove is the best and does not absorb water.
- Lanyard for tippet, snips, etc.
- Handheld GPS to mark your favorite river spots.
- High intensity headlamp.
- Insect repellent and poison ivy/oak block for summer steelhead and early salmon.
- Salt and shovel in automobile. Also flares/blankets/jumper cables.
- First-aid kit and moisturizing cream.
- Line cleaner.
- Wader-repair kit.
- Boga-grip or similar scale. Also a tape measure.
- A waterproof Pelican case to protect cameras.
- Cell phone for emergencies.
- Choose a vest or vest pack that meets your storage and style preference needs. There are so many excellent ones on the market.
- Read every book, article, DNR report, etc., on the salmon/steelhead experience. It's a lifetime learning curve.
- Hang out at diners, bars, and motels that other salmon/steelhead anglers frequent. Keep your ears open and be willing to share information and advice. Don't just talk to fly guys. Bait/hardware fishers are lethal fishermen and sometimes have generations of knowledge.

- Don't be greedy—enjoy each salmon and steelhead experience. "Blessed are the meek, patient and humble, for yours will be salmonid nirvana!"
- Tell your guide what your skill level is, how you want to fish or what you want to learn, and what your goal is for the trip. Don't be afraid to ask "stupid" questions.
- Stay very focused on each cast and presentation of the fly. You must anticipate striking silver, and you must be in the "meditation of the grab!"
- Visualize and study the holding lies and river structure by taking time-outs from casting and studying the water and flow.
- Enjoy the flora and fauna of your environment—breathe in the sounds, scents, and sights of the river.
- Keep it jovial and light—enjoy the camaraderie of your partners.
- Don't expect to catch fish on every trip, especially when dealing with ocean-run salmonids that don't have to eat if they don't want to.
- Have fun and experiment with different fly patterns and enjoy inventing some personal fly patterns—this is probably the best part of our sport.
- If you break a fish off, learn from your mistakes. Ask a friend or guide what you did wrong. Experience builds character and a better salmon/steelheader.

4

PRESENTATION AND THE FLY

Casting and presentation are art forms that develop through practice.

By combining the fundamental techniques of presentation with learning how to read the rivers where Great Lakes salmon and steelhead are found, as well as understanding the behavior of the fish under all conditions, total mastery is attained.

The proper presentation is a function of the best method for the conditions, time of year, fish species pursued and its behavior, along with personal preferred fishing style. As with all art forms, there is not one absolute method a person must use. The successful salmon/steelheader has an open mind for creativity and experimentation. Redundancy of technique and fly patterns often leads to conditioned behavioral responses by the salmonids, and they avoid being hooked and almost become bored to tears by the angler's habitual lack of creativity. How often do we get stuck using the same drift and flies, when along comes someone who, either out of sheer dumb luck or purposeful intention, pulls some odd looking fly out of the box and casts it in an unconventional way and—voilà!—catches a large fish. These humbling encounters show the enigmatic aspects of salmon/steelheading, and how one must learn the basics and then improvise for success.

BOTTOM DRIFT NYMPHING—CHUCK-AND-DUCK

This has become the classic presentation for the cold water Great Lakes salmonid angler. With the rig described in the tackle chapter, the cast uses lead weight to propel the thin running/shooting line and penetrate the swift, cold waters immediately. The cast is usually executed by swinging the weight and flies behind the angler. On the "water load," the weight touches the water for a fraction of a second to load the rod tip. With a snap of the wrist, the line is propelled to the desired point of entry into the water as the rod tip follows through in the same direction. With one or two slack-line upstream mends of the rod, the lead and flies are allowed to sink to the bottom and the egg and nymph

The bottom-drift (chuck-and-duck) technique is easy for novice salmon and steelhead anglers to learn. Here, it allowed Jared Adler to take this beautiful steelhead in front of the Gray Drake Lodge on Michigan's Muskegon River.

patterns bounce along the bottom drag free. When fishing deep pools and runs with this method, all of the angler's focus should be on the rod tip. A steady bouncing of the tip indicates contact with the bottom, which is the desire of this method. If the tip droops very slowly, a snag on the bottom has occurred. By lifting the rod slowly upstream and pulling very gently on the line, 90 percent of all snags can be eliminated and the terminal tackle saved. If the angler sets the hook on a snag, it is certain he will lose the whole rig. So when does the angler set the hook? By watching the rod tip very closely;

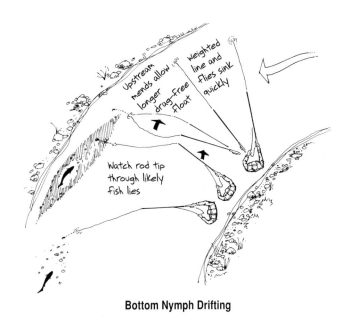

Upstream mends allow longer drag-free float

Weighted line and flies sink quickly

Watch rod tip through likely fish lies

Bottom Nymph Drifting

the sudden throbbing of the tip will signal the fly being struck and the salmonid shaking its head to dislodge the fly. The fly usually hooks the fish with the force of the water's current. A quick strip set and a sharp hook will ensure contact.

In order for the line to penetrate the water at the desired 90-degree angle, hold the rod handle straight out at 9:30 or 2:30 (clock positions). This keeps as much line off the water as possible, which reduces unwanted drag. Holding the rod too high will create more slack. The goal is to lift line and create tightness of feel to detect strikes.

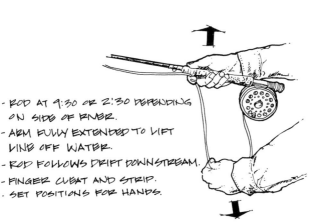

- ROD AT 9:30 OR 2:30 DEPENDING ON SIDE OF RIVER.
- ARM FULLY EXTENDED TO LIFT LINE OFF WATER.
- ROD FOLLOWS DRIFT DOWNSTREAM.
- FINGER CLEAT AND STRIP.
- SET POSITIONS FOR HANDS.

Bottom Drift Technique

To penetrate deep lies, a more upstream cast is needed. In shallower runs and lies, use a down-and-across approach. If your rod tip is not bouncing, you are not on the bottom and must feed out more line. This method is very effective for fishing egg patterns, nymphs, small wets, and streamers for fall salmon, steelhead, and lake-run browns, and for winter and spring steelheading. It can also be used to swing flies through pools for early holding chinook salmon. When fishing the pools and runs for holding fall and winter steelhead, a "slip-sinker" weight system that slides up and down the leader is desired. This is best for deeper and slower waters that lack the current of the faster runs and gravel areas. Also, this method allows steelhead to inhale the fly and not feel the weight, giving the angler more time to set the hook.

In shallow spawning gravel and runs, quick strike detection is required. A three-way swivel is used where the leader is attached to one eye, a dropper weight off the second, and the fly or flies off the third eye. When fishing gravel spawning runs, the angler's eye turns away from the rod tip and now focuses on the line. A sudden stopping of the line usually signals a mouth grab by a salmon or steelhead—a quick hook-set is usually required. This technique is effective for fall chinooks, lake-run browns, and spring steelhead on or near gravel.

A 20-pound St. Mary's summer Atlantic salmon taken by strike-indicator nymphing a scud pattern.

STRIKE-INDICATOR NYMPHING

Strike-indicator nymphing is becoming ever more popular with anglers wanting to use floating fly lines without massive amounts of lead and running lines. The technique is best used in moderate to shallower rivers and streams, or on or near gravel spawning areas. A single- or double-handed Spey rod may be used. A weight-forward floating or salmon/ steelhead taper line is used. By using the leader described earlier in the tackle section, the sliding strike indicator is placed first on the leader, followed by the fly or flies (in states that allow two-fly rigs.) The split shot can be applied in two areas. Many anglers prefer it 6 to 12 inches

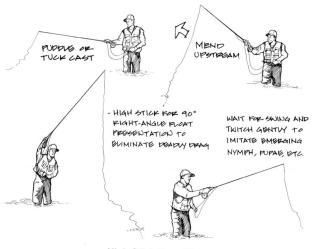

PUDDLE OR TUCK CAST

MEND UPSTREAM

- HIGH STICK FOR 90°
RIGHT-ANGLE FLOAT
PRESENTATION TO
ELIMINATE DEADLY DRAG

WAIT FOR SWING AND
TWITCH GENTLY TO
IMITATE EMERGING
NYMPH, PUPAE, ETC.

High Stick Nymphing

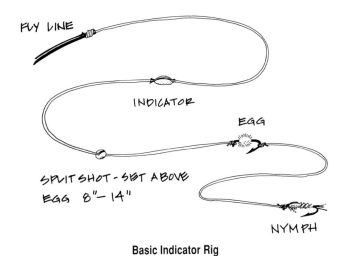

Basic Indicator Rig

above the fly. In the "panfish" style rig, the split shot is applied at the very bottom—below the flies. However, to be legal, the flies must have a three-inch tag off the main leader—dropper style. I personally prefer this rig because it is easier to accurately set the strike indicator to ensure that the flies are in the proper strike zone. As a general rule, the indicator is usually set one and a half to two times the depth you are fishing.

The "Indy" or indicator rig uses a floating line, strike indicator, nymphs/egg patterns, and split shot to provide a near-bottom, drag-free presentation. The strikes are detected by the indicator bobbing down. In addition, the indicator provides a 90-degree angle presentation that induces less drag.

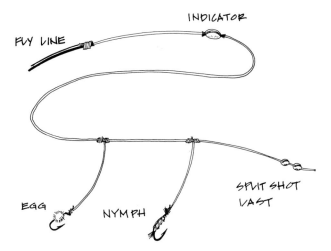

FLY LINE

INDICATOR

EGG

NYMPH

SPLIT SHOT VAST

NOTE: EGG AND FLY MUST HAVE 3" TAG OFF THE MAIN TIPPET LINE

Panfish-Style Indicator Rig

Executing the "Indy" rig method is best achieved by using longer rods or Spey rods that get additional lifting of the line off the water for drag-free floats. The effect is similar to cane-pole bobber fishing. Setting the weight or split shot is determined by the depth and speed of the current. During the drift, you want to eliminate any belly in the line that might create drag. A proper float of the rig should be slower than the current, and the strike indicator should be ticking ever so slightly to show that the flies and shot are drifting close to the bottom. If you hang up on snags, you are in the ballpark—a slight shortening up of the strike indicator will fine tune the presentation. Your rod should be high-sticked over the strike indicator as it moves downstream with continuous drag-free mends. Set the hook each time the bobber dips below the water. The most common strikes are a steady underwater pull in a sideward direction from the indicator, or a quick take as the indicator takes off fast.

Indicator rigs are very effective for fishing to salmon and steelhead in shallow-water gravel runs. They are also preferred for pool and pocket-water fishing on moderate to smaller rivers containing lots of wooded debris where bottom drift nymphing creates a snag-filled proposition. Michigan's Pere Marquette River is an excellent river for this technique.

CLASSIC DOWN-AND-ACROSS SWING

This traditional Atlantic salmon and West Coast steelhead technique is very deadly on Great Lakes salmonids. Sinking-tip or intermediate lines are used when presenting Spey wets or streamers in faster, deeper runs and tail-outs and pools. A floating line can be used with some weight incorporated in the head of the fly for smaller river and stream presentations.

The basic objective is to present a wet fly swinging crosscurrent to pique the interest of a fresh-run salmon or steelhead. The technique is best executed by a parachute or puddle cast. The check cast is stopped similarly to the puddle cast, and by zigzagging the tip to

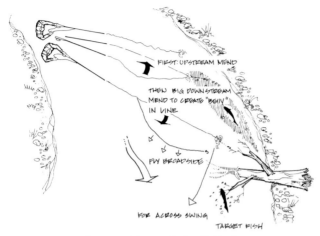

Down-and-Across Swing Method

produce snake-like coils. Proper depth penetration is achieved with constant up- and downstream mending.

The key is to envision the holding lies that you believe the fish are occupying. The downstream, broadside drift should be executing its swing slightly upstream of the taking lies, and then swing through them. To start, position yourself upstream of the holding lies. Mend the cast several times upstream for depth penetration; follow with a long downstream mend to create a belly of line that is tight to the reel and allows for the swing. Strikes are often violent, with the fish hooking itself—keep drags set lightly. With the clockwork method, which breaks the pool run down from 9 to 3 o'clock, each quadrant of the pool can be fished as the angler progressively moves down the run and casts to the envisioned clock position.

Keep in mind that this technique is most effective under ideal water with a clear to slight strain, and river temperatures between 40 and 60 degrees F.

DEEP-DRIFT SINKING-LINE TECHNIQUES

This is a very effective method, especially when our Great Lakes rivers are running cold, high, and off-color. Pioneered by Trey Combs and Lani Waller on the fast-flowing British Columbia rivers, it will get a large Spey wet fly or streamer down and deep in the strike zone for a long time. Use a sinking-tip or full-

This female Atlantic salmon was taken from a large pool using deep-sinking-line techniques. She was fooled by a chartreuse Candy Cane Leech.

sinking line at the various weights 200 to 600 grains, or Class II to VII combined with a short 3- to 5-foot-long leader to the fly. These custom-made depth–charge lines either have long bellies in either floating, intermediate, or running varieties. By executing a series of up, down, and stack mends, the angler can control the sink rate, depth penetration, and hang time of the drift.

To execute the presentation, one must first focus on the holding and taking lies of the salmonids, whether it be the pocket waters, pool/gut/flats, or tail-out. The goal is to envision where the fish will be, and to focus on slowing down the fly's swing and keep it in the prime strike zones as long as possible. Position yourself above the lies you are about to fish. Start upstream and throw roll casts or slack line at the point of entry

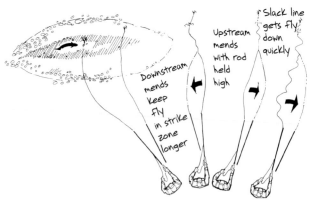

Deep Sink Tip Presentation

where the line meets the water to allow the fly to sink. The amount of slack line to add to your presentation is dictated by how fast and deep the water is flowing. As you make mend adjustments, keep the line tight enough to feel a strike, which is often slow and sluggish in the cold, high-water conditions. Keep the rod high and upstream to create tension and maximum depth penetration. As you use heavier sinking tips, you'll lose strike detection. Set the hook on any quirky movement of the line. Practicing this technique makes for perfection. This technique is most effective for late-fall and winter steelheading when the fish are hunkered down in the guts of the pools and runs. Ten-foot, 8-weight rods, or Spey rods, work best to handle the long mends and deal with heavy lines.

SPEY AND DRY-FLY TECHNIQUES

The Spey-rod revolution has taken a strong hold in the Great Lakes, and is a very practical technique for swinging flies or strike-indicator nymphing. One can utilize the single or double Spey cast, the overhead cast, which is nothing more than a double-handed style single-handed fly cast, or the various specialty casts like the snap-T, snake roll, and underhand cast. A book could be filled just describing the casts, thus I suggest studying the various Spey instructional videos on the market or taking a Spey-casting school with a reputable instructor. The most practical presentation with a floating or sinking-tip Spey line is the classic double Spey.

John Miller executes a snap-T Spey cast on Michigan's lower Muskegon River. Wide Great Lakes rivers are ideal for Spey casting.

With the fly anchored below you, the rod and line are swept upstream in a back-handed roll cast as the right hand leads the rod (in an over-the-right-shoulder double Spey) and the left hand is held firmly to the right side of the chest. As the fly and line lay in the water downstream with an upstream triangle of rod and line formed, a quick sideways sweeping D-shaped cast is made to the downstream, right side of the angler. This allows the direction change to take place for the final step. With a fluid push/pull of the forward cast, the right hand is held high above the head, keeping the rod tip high and stopping it to execute delivery. The tight loop Spey then sails up and across the river.

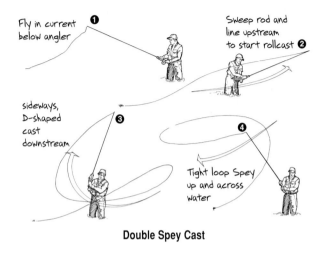

Fly in current below angler ❶

Sweep rod and line upstream to start rollcast ❷

sideways, D-shaped cast downstream ❸

Tight loop Spey up and across water ❹

Double Spey Cast

The beauty of two-handed Spey rod presentations lies in the fact that you can cover vast amounts of water, have long-distance line control by mending, cast through a steep canyon or where a bank does not allow for a back cast, and have a tremendous amount of hang time on the tail of your drifts where the fly can be manipulated to swim by pumping and swaying the rod.

A dry-fly presentation is becoming more popular in the Great Lakes, especially for steelhead, lake-run browns and Atlantic salmon. To date, it has had its greatest success on the shallower Lake Erie tributaries like the Cattaraugus of New York and Ontario's Grand and Maitland Rivers. Tom Kurowski, of Buffalo Outfitters, authors Rick and Jerry Kustich, Ontario guide John

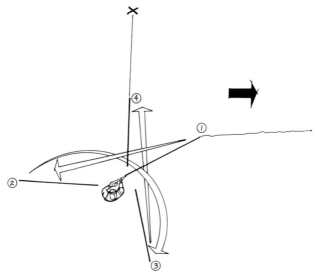

Top View of Double Spey Cast

Valk, and biologist Larry Halyk have been pioneering dry-fly techniques with good success. However, as with all dry presentations to salmonids, timing, water conditions, and persistence (and a lot of luck) play a major role. It is far from a consistent proposition.

Due to the sheer numbers of steelhead present in these tributaries from heavy stockings, the chrome and aggressive autumn fish will stack into pools and runs, and display territorial holding behavior that is conducive to striking a dry. Most strikes occur by waking a dry on a Riffle Hitch, West Coast style, or by twitching a dead-drift presentation.

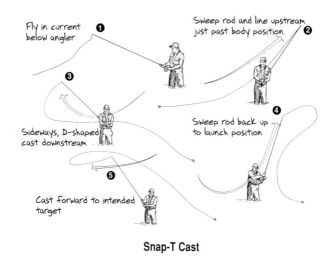

Snap-T Cast

1. Fly in current below angler
2. Sweep rod and line upstream just past body position
3. Sideways, D-shaped cast downstream
4. Sweep rod back up to launch position
5. Cast forward to intended target

Other dry-fly scenarios exist during late spring when drop-back steelhead encounter massive aquatic insect emergers such as gray and brown drakes and *Isonychia*. This occurs in late May on large insect-rich rivers. Michigan's Muskegon, Pere Marquette, and Big Manistee and Ontario's Grand and Maitland Rivers are prime examples. In these cases the steelhead are feeding—chasing and ingesting the flies on their way back down to Lake Michigan. I have personally experienced these feeding fish. As for Atlantic salmon in the Salmon River of New York and Michigan/Ontario's St. Mary's, waking and dead drifting dries at first light can often bring about explosive strikes or boiling refusals. When the *Hexagenia* hatch is in full swing on

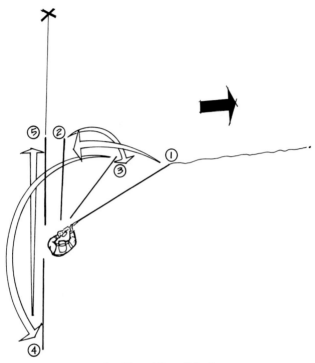

Top View of Snap-T Cast

the St. Mary's, the Atlantics will target and feed on the adults and emergers. Finally, on several Lake Superior tributaries like the Bois Brule of Wisconsin, which attract August runs of lake-run browns, many anglers successfully pursue them at dusk using deer-hair mice and other large dry flies.

A dime-bright chinook salmon taken in August.

TECHNIQUES FOR POOLED-UP PACIFIC SALMON

Unique, early Pacific salmon runs exist on the cold, spring-fed waters of Michigan's Little Manistee and Pere Marquette, along with the Lake Superior–fed St. Mary's rapids. Chrome-silver chinook salmon enter these rivers as early as July and August after a good cold front brings ample rains and cools the waters further. Usually, by late August and early September, the large, deep pools of large chinook rivers like New York's Salmon and Michigan's Big Manistee and Muskegon will be loaded with schools of tail-slapping, surface-boiling fish. It is quite a spectacle to see hundreds of fish, pent up in pools and swimming around in pods. They tend to favor the deepest pools; on the

Muskegon and Big Manistee that could mean water 12 to 20 feet deep.

These fish, "not ready and ripe enough" to spawn, have perplexed salmon anglers for decades. They often come in on rising water levels and pool up when waters recede. Still, at times, fall water temperatures heat up during a warm spell and drive the salmon down deep and off the spawn. Understanding their behavior is the key to catching these fish on a fly rod. Since they are not eating, aggression and territorial dominance is their main cue. First light and dusk show the most porpoising, jumping, tail-slapping, and boiling at the surface by the fish. The key is that these fish are hovering in the pool, suspended from the bottom to the surface. Bottom drifting a fly is futile. One must swing or drift to these fish at various suspended depths. At first light or dusk, fish bright chartreuse, orange, black, and gold Comet/Boss imitations. As light approaches, switch to dull-colored nymphs and small baitfish streamers. The Bead-Chain Boss and Comet, West Coast patterns, show an uncanny ability to agitate pooled-up Pacifics. The action could be fast and furious—or dead. Swinging flies on sinking-tips (clear intermediates preferred) or chuck-and-duck style will be effective. Inclement weather with rain seems to be the best producer.

LAKE TROUT AND COASTER BROOK TROUT

One of the only true indigenous salmonids of the char family in the Great Lakes, the lake trout still pros-

A coaster brook trout is always a special catch. This one was taken on Scott Smith's Green-Butt Monkey in Lake Superior's Cypress River.

pers quite well due to the help of the U.S. Fish & Wildlife Service and many of the Great Lakes states and province of Ontario's stringent management regulations. It is found in all the Great Lakes in substantial numbers, except for perhaps Lake Erie. The coaster brook trout, on the other hand, is now strictly limited in its native range to the northern shore of Lake Superior (Nipigon District), with a slow but steady resurgence in micro populations on Lake Superior's south shore. This fish is being studied and managed carefully in an effort to restore populations throughout its historic range.

The lake trout is a strong baitfish predator, and favors deeper waters and low-light conditions. It will also spawn along rocky reefs and shorelines, often foregoing river migration during fall spawning cycles. Good numbers of spawning fish ascend Michigan's Grand River and New York/Ontario's Niagara to create a visible trophy fishery. Any given river during the fall on Lakes Superior, Huron, Michigan, and Ontario could see a sporadic school of these fish. As with all of the char family, they are extremely non-selective eaters and are very gullible to fly presentations. White and chartreuse Zuddlers, baitfish streamers, and chartreuse Glo-bugs will hook many fish. Their fight is very dogged, deep throbbing like a giant brown. They can be a lot of fun on the fly rod.

The coaster brook trout of Ontario's Nipigon/Thunder Bay district are very large, thick-girthed creatures with the magnificent color display of a resident stream brookie. They run the Cypress River as early as late July, and usually peak around late August. Good rains always bring in a fresh batch of fish, averaging 3 to 5 pounds. They are extremely aggressive when they take the fly. They are very strong fighters, and equally important is their radiant spawning-color beauty. Rabbit strip Zonker-style streamers in chartreuse, white, olive, and beige tones produce best. Scott Smith, the regional coaster brook trout expert and guide, ties a Green-Butt Monkey streamer that is deadly; I can personally attest to twenty hook-up days for these magnificent fish when the run is on.

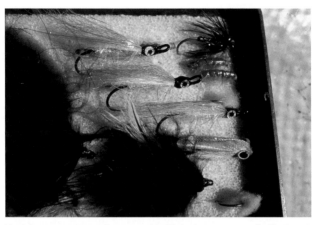

Nymphs, egg patterns, Speys, and baitfish streamers are all effective at times for Great Lakes salmonids.

A GREAT LAKES SALMON/STEELHEAD FLY BOX

From the hallowed Atlantic salmon rivers of Scotland to the wild majesty of British Columbia's steelhead Valhalla, a colorful, intriguing and artistic fly-tying tradition has evolved. Though the Great Lakes salmonid fishery is fairly new in comparison, it has made great innovations in a short period of time.

To beguile a salmon or steelhead to strike the fly takes confidence in one's pattern, persistence in presentation, patience and an effervescent state of mental optimism. The age-old enigma of why a migratory salmonid strikes the fly will amuse the ocean-run fish advocate and fill the angler's perplexing diaries and hard fought riverside experience for a lifetime. Natal imprinting to food forms, aggression, territorial dominance, and a programmed genetic urge to strike when provoked, based on an evolutionary predator/prey response behavior, sums up the experiences with our quarry.

If there is any variance from the anadromous (ocean to fresh water) behavioral disposition of Pacific and Atlantic salmonids, it must lie in the simplicity of the

Curt Collins with a chrome St. Mary's Atlantic salmon that took an emerging caddis pupae. Sometimes it pays to try different patterns, particularly on hard-fished rivers.

PRESENTATION AND THE FLY

complete freshwater lifecycle found in the Great Lakes. Living a potamadromous (fresh water to fresh water) life may alleviate some of the physiological complications of adjusting to salinity when migrating, and may indeed enhance the ability of these fish to eat food—and flies—on a longer and more sustained basis. Special regard must be given to the biological richness and complexity of food in the Great Lakes and its river ecosystems. Baitfish such as alewives, herring, chubs, emerald shiners, gobies, and shad are evolving in density and being enhanced with new exotic species entering the system, having both positive and negative impacts. Aquatic and terrestrial insects, along with *Mysis* and *Diporeia* shrimp, round out the food chain. Where significant natural reproduction of salmon and steelhead populations exists, particularly in Lakes Superior, Michigan, Huron, and Ontario, one can walk the riverbanks and see the baby salmonid fry feverishly feeding on the emerging midges, mayflies, and stoneflies, a conditioned learned response at this early developmental stage. Compared to the significantly more food sterile environments on some of the Western rivers, the Great Lakes are a food factory for salmonids.

If anything novel exists about Great Lakes salmonid fly patterns, it is in the tremendous diversity and complexity of offerings that the angler must be well versed in.

NYMPH AND EGG PATTERNS

These form the "meat and potatoes" of the salmon and steelhead fisheries fly box. Based on the massive

The late great Ohio steelhead guide Dr. Mike Bennet searches for the perfect egg pattern from his well-stocked sucker spawn box.

density of aquatic insects, along with salmonid and sucker eggs in the river's biological drift, patterns are selected and modified with both naturalistic and impressionistic motifs. The first nymphal patterns, like Michigan's Spring Wiggler, were developed off the Brindle/Woolly Worm concept. These shell-back flies imitate the *Hexagenia limbata*. With a tremendous diversity of mayflies, stoneflies, caddis, and shrimp in the river systems, nymph imitations should be based on these food forms.

SUGGESTED NYMPHS

- Green caddis larvae—#8–16
- *Hexagenia* (Hex)—#4–8
- Oliver Edwards's black stone and other black and golden stonefly—#8–12
- Black & purple Disco Stone and Prince—#8–14
- Hare's Ear—#6–14
- Gartside Sparrow—#6–12
- *Mysis* shrimp and scuds—#8–16
- Alevin sac-fry—#6–8
- Steelhead Hammer—#10–12
- Polish Woven—#10–12
- Czech-mate—#10–12
- Quill/peacock soft hackle—#8–14
- Bead-head Pheasant Tail—#8–16

The egg pattern has evolved from the simple Glo-bug pioneered by Anderson, of California's Bug Shop, to highly specialized patterns using yarn with flashy synthetic materials like Estaz. The sheer volume of eggs being extruded by spawning salmon, steelhead, suckers, walleye, etc., make them the number-one choice of all Great Lakes fly anglers. It is important to know the metamorphosis and colors of the natural egg. chinook, coho, pink, and Atlantic salmon, along with steelhead, have a more orange/yellow tint. Sucker spawn is caviar, small and bright yellow. The metamorphosis of an egg, once it is free flowing in the river, goes from the orange/yellow to a paler cream to almost a purplish/blue color in its final stages of decay—thus the appeal lately of blue egg patterns.

Suggested Egg Patterns

- Glo-bugs—all sizes and colors—#6–18
- Nuke eggs—#8–16
- Sucker spawn or cluster weaves—#8–16

Note: Eggs can be enhanced by adding Krystal Flash, Flashabou, Mylar Motion, and other glitter.

Wets, Speys, Tubes, Streamers, and Dry Flies

This group incorporates the traditional Atlantic salmon and West Coast steelhead patterns with baitfish motifs, which allows for ultimate creative expression. The first Great Lakes wets, as tried by the Richey brothers of Michigan and early trout guides on the Pere Marquette like Zimmy Nolph, incorporated West Coast brightly colored motifs. These flies, which are

The wide variety of fly-tying materials now available makes it easy for salmon and steelhead anglers to experiment with new patterns.

meant to be swung on the down-and-across drift, trigger aggression, playfulness, curiosity, as well as the desire to eat baitfish. Dries are meant to be waked on a Riffle Hitch down-and-across pools and tail-outs, or dead drifted and twitched in faster pocket water.

SUGGESTED WETS

- Winter Hope—#4–10
- Burlap—#6–10
- Micro Signal Light and Freight Train—#6–12
- Golden Demon—#4–6
- Macks Canyon—#4–8
- Purple Peril—#2–8

- Purple polar bear Matuka—#2–6
- Christmas Trinity—#4–6
- Washougal Olive—#4–6

SPEY FLIES

- Sol Duc series—#2/0–6
- Picasse—#2–8
- Marabou Paintbrush—#2–6
- Bronze Brad's Brat—#2–8
- Marabou Popsicle series—#2/0–6
- Thugmeister—#2/0–8
- September Spey—#2–6
- Tequilla Sunrise—#2–6
- Steelhead Stinger—#2/0–4
- Steelhead Ackroyd—#2/0–4

TUBE FLIES

- Willie Gunn—1–2 inches
- Temple Dog—1–2 inches
- Tippet Shrimp—1–2 inches
- Maygog Smelt—1–2 inches

STREAMERS/MATUKAS/BUCKTAILS

- Egg-Sucking Leech—#2–10
- Halo Harlot—#2–4
- Steelhead Woolly Bugger—#4–10
- Bunny Bugger—#2/0–4
- Leechsicle—#2/0–4
- Comet/Boss—#4–6

The surf and open waters of the Great Lakes are fast becoming an important fishery for fly anglers.

- Opossum Sculpin—#2–6
- Tasmanian Sculpin—#2/0–4
- White Cone-head Zuddler—#2–4
- C-4 See Me Alewife and Smelt—#2/0–4
- Electric Candy Cane—#2/0–4
- Muddler Minnow—#2–8
- Stickleback Sculpin—#2–6

DRY FLIES

- White & Red Wulff—#4–8
- Steelhead Bee—#4–6
- Waller Wakers—#4–8
- Steelhead Caddis—#6–8

An angler probes a run for salmon and steelhead on a crisp autumn day while a black lab checks out dying chinook salmon near shore.

Autumn

Salmon in pools: Comets and Boss, Speys and larger nymphs.

Salmon on gravel: Nymphs, eggs, and Woolly Bugger/Muddler/Matukas; Egg-Sucking Leeches.

Lake-run browns and coaster brook trout: Light egg patterns; white Zuddlers; olive and black Matukas; bushy nymphs.

Steelhead: Baitfish and sculpin style streamers; fluorescent Speys and wets; egg patterns; Woolly Buggers; white Zuddlers; Hex nymphs.

Winter

Steelhead: Micro Nuke Eggs; stonefly, Hare's Ear, Hex, and green caddis nymphs; olive and gray sculpins; baitfish patterns in river estuaries; purple and blue Disco Stone and Prince Nymphs; Mysis shrimp; Steelhead Hammer.

Spring

Steelhead in pools and on gravel: Alevin sac-fry nymphs; various egg fly imitations; Sparrow, Hex, green caddis, Hare's Ear, stonefly, Disco Prince and Mysis shrimp nymph; Steelhead Woolly Buggers and fluorescent Speys.

Drop-back steelhead: Various baitfish imitations, salmon fry patterns, and mayfly emergers.

Face to face with a chrome fall steelhead.

Summer

Atlantic salmon: Smelt/shiner baitfish patterns; natural and yellow Muddlers; caddis, shrimp, and Hex nymphs; Wulff, Adams Irresistible, and Bomber dries; Stickly Sculpins; small classic salmon wets.

Summer steelhead: Alewife baitfish and white Zuddlers; fluorescent Leechsicles; Tasmanian Sculpins; Thugmeister; black/blue/purple Speys and leeches; Electric Candy-Cane Bunny Buggers.

Early King Salmon in Pools: Comets and Boss, Egg-Sucking Leeches, chartreuse and orange Speys.

Peter and Matt Supinski with a late-summer chrome chinook salmon from Lake Michigan.

Late-summer lake-run browns and coaster brook trout: Olive leeches and sculpins; smelt/herring baitfish patterns; white Zuddlers; mottled yellow, gold, and red Muddlers; deer-hair mice and yellow Wulff dries.

HOW TO HOOK, FIGHT, AND LAND SALMON AND STEELHEAD

Perhaps the most exciting aspect of salmon and steelhead on the fly is the spectacular fighting performance of these fish. Their spectacular aerial leaps, hard thrashing runs, and bearish refusal to submit will keep the angler addicted to the ocean-run fish for life.

The tremendous leaping ability of summer Skamania steelhead will test an angler's fighting skills.

The strike and hook-set vary with each encounter, time of year, species, fly presentation, and fly pattern. Strikes can be rod-throbbing smashes, subtle head-shakes, or pauses in the drift. Newly migrated fish that haven't seen a lot of pressure usually crush the fly due to their lack of caution. This often occurs on the down-and-across swing method, and when bottom-drifting egg patterns, when the current hooks the fish as it takes the fly on a broadside presentation. In winter bottom-drift (chuck-and-duck) or strike-indicator nymphing, strikes can be subtle, especially in coldwater conditions and when using small nymphs or eggs. When casting to fish on gravel, the line stopping in the drift often signals that the fly has been intercepted. Regardless, a firm strip-set downstream of the fish will drive the hook home. On the bony mouth of a kyped male salmon or steelhead, the firmer the hook-set, the better, but don't overdo it or your fish will break off.

Once the fish is on, carefully reel the loose line onto the reel as you pinch the line with your other hand to keep tension. Not enough tension in the line at the onset of the fight will allow a fish to shake the fly free. Often, a hooked fish will charge, and you'll be stripping or reel scrambling to maintain tension. The best way to ensure proper tension is to drop your rod tip a foot or so below the water. This will allow the water to provide resistance on the line to the running fish. Once contact is made, let the fish run on the reel's drag system. On direct-drive reels, don't touch the handle or allow it or the spool rim to hit your clothing, vest, etc. Keep a bow in the rod, pointing it in the direction of the fish. If the fish jumps, bow to it with the rod to release the drag system quickly. By constantly changing rod direction to the 9 o'clock and 3 o'clock horizontal positions, you'll tire a fish and confuse its equilibrium orientation quicker. If the fish drives left, your rod should sweep laterally to the right, and vice versa.

Once you're ready to land the fish, be aware that it will make one last run when it sees the net or your tailing hand. Some fish play possum and then—wham!— a quick break-off occurs. Bottom line: stay focused throughout the fight—it ain't over till it's over! Lighting of cigars, flashing cameras, and nips from the flask come after the fish is landed—not during the battle.

Thanks to new equipment and techniques, more fly fishers are now targeting the Great Lakes surf.

Photograph your fish quickly, revive it carefully by using a tailing glove, and enjoy the experience.

SURF-FISHING GREAT LAKES SALMONID

This is a new and exciting frontier for the Great Lakes fly fisher. As river conditions become more crowded and water levels unpredictable, and with the sheer predator aggression that big lake salmonids possess, the lure to target these fish "in the surf" is compelling. And with the pioneering work done by innovative saltwater anglers, fly casting in the surf is now a very productive option.

Pacific and Atlantic salmon, steelhead, lake trout, and brown and coaster brook trout can be pursued on a seasonal basis. During the late winter and spring, coho, chinook, Atlantics, lake trout, and browns will be found off the pier-heads of tributary rivers, and off warmwater electrical and nuclear discharge. The amount of baitfish schooling near these areas will be significant. Alewives, smelt, shiners, and shad will use these areas due to the warmer water flows and also as a pre-spawning gathering place. Surf anglers should look for onshore winds, which bring in the warmer offshore waters in the 40-degree Fahrenheit range. A gentle chop and overcast days are ideal. Look for porpoising salmonids along with seagulls herding baitfish. Fish the rocks and drop-off ledges where the river channels empty into the big lake. Also concentrate on the line marking the boundary between the clear lake water and the cloudier river water. Double-haul sinking lines on

A fat, chrome male chinook from Lake Michigan's surf.

one- or two-handed rods with very large baitfish streamer patterns. Target moving schools of salmonids by casting in front of the prowling fish. Be prepared for a jolting strike and aerial battle like you've never seen!

Summer brings on the greatest surf opportunities with summer Skamania steelhead. Since the fish's natal rivers often run hot and dry, these July/August river-run fish will often stack up along the pier-head river estuaries. The key to this occurrence are offshore winds, which will push the warm beach temperatures, often averaging 75 to 80 degrees F, out into the big lake and bring in a cold undertow of cold interior lake water. Beach temperatures can drop to the upper 40s and lower 50s with sustainable offshore winds, creating a summer steelhead and alewife baitfish "surfs-up" magic carpet ride. If river temperatures remain hot, the river-sick Skamanias will stage for days or weeks, foraging on alewives. Surf and pier casting with a Spey rod or trolling can be extremely productive. Early dawn and dusk periods are recommended. Target schools of seagulls, and watch for surface-boiling alewives and seagulls on the hunt. Bright chartreuse, orange, and pink bunny Leechsicles are hot producers at the low-light levels of dusk and dawn.

Late summer will find chinook, coho and pink salmon in the surf. Once again, the key is a brisk offshore wind, and low and warm rivers that will keep the fish beach-bound. These fish are noted for incredible circle-schooling behavior. Target the stragglers and you'll often find curious fish that want to take a baitfish imitation.

Finally, autumn brings in lake trout and browns, along with roaming fall steelhead looking for food. Though baitfish patterns work well, dead-drifting cluster egg patterns is the choice since the rivers will be emanating the sexual scent of spawning Pacific salmon and their smorgasbord of dislodged unfertilized eggs.

GETTING TO THE FISH

Whether to wade, or use a drift boat, jet sled, or pontoon/belly boat is a matter of personal choice. If you wade, make sure you know the water, its level, and crossing-point areas well. Drift boats are ideal for covering large distances of river and can put you onto holes and runs too deep to wade. Jet sleds can further

This lake-run brown trout was fooled by a streamer.

PRESENTATION AND THE FLY

increase your advantage, allowing you to go up- and downstream, draft in 6 inches of water, and open up your game plan for the river on a daily basis. Pontoon boats are great for smaller boulder-strewn rivers and shallow tight-water streams. Belly boats are becoming popular; however, they can be dangerous on fast-flowing, ice-cold waters.

Do your homework, get advice on the waters you fish, and use common safety sense in all of your endeavors. Be courteous to both boat and wading anglers, and give them space. The waters are becoming much too crowded and etiquette can go a long way.

5

A GUIDE TO BLUE-RIBBON GREAT LAKES SALMON/STEELHEAD RIVERS

The following is a list of choice Great Lakes salmonid rivers, each with a species guide and several access points.

LAKE SUPERIOR

Michigan

St. Mary's River—Chinook, coho, and pink salmon; Atlantic salmon; fall through spring steelhead; lake-run brown trout.
Access: American/Canadian Rapids, Sault Edison Plant.
Big Two-Hearted River—Chinook and coho salmon, fall through spring steelhead, lake-run brown trout.
Access: Coast Guard Road, East Branch.
Big Huron River—Chinook salmon, fall through spring steelhead, lake-run browns.
Access: Big Eric's Bridge, West Branch Huron Road.
Chocolay River—Chinook, coho, and pink salmon; fall through spring steelhead; splake; and lake-run browns.
Access: M28, County Road 480. (Note: The Cherry Creek tributary still receives wild runs of summer steelhead from discontinued hatchery stockings.)

129

Ontonagon River—Chinook and coho salmon, fall through spring steelhead, lake-run browns.
Access: Military Bridge to Victoria Road.

Wisconsin

Bois Brule River—Chinook and coho salmon, fall through spring steelhead, lake-run browns.
Access: Below Highway 2—Mays and Leynroot Ledges, Pine Tree Landing, Grass Eddy.

Minnesota

Knife River—Chinook, coho, and pink salmon; fall through spring steelhead; Kamloops rainbow trout.
Access: County Roads 42, 41, 11, 9.
Devil Track River—Coho and pink salmon, fall through spring steelhead.
Access: SR 61, County Road 12.
Temperance River—Chinook, coho, and pink salmon; fall through spring steelhead.
Access: County Road 2, FR 166, 164.
Baptism River—Coho and pink salmon, fall through spring steelhead.
Access: SR 61, County Road 6, 7, and 1.

Ontario

Nipigon River—Chinook, coho, and pink salmon; coaster brook trout; spring and summer steelhead.

Jay Edelstein and the author with a St. Mary's Atlantic salmon. The pronounced kype makes it easy to identify the fish as a male.

Access: Alexander's Dam, Trans Canada Highway 585.

Jack Pine River—Coho, lake trout, coaster brook trout, pink salmon, fall and spring steelhead.

Access: Trans Canada Highway upstream 15 kilometers to first barrier.

Cypress River—Coho and pink salmon, lake trout, coaster brook trout, fall and spring steelhead.

Access: Trans Canada Highway upstream by trail paths.

Steel River—Chinook, coho, and pink salmon; coaster brook trout; fall, spring, and summer steelhead.

Access: Trans Canada Highway upstream to the falls at Santoy Lake.

Michipicoton River—Chinook, coho, and pink salmon; fall, spring, and summer steelhead.

Access: Scott Falls Power Dam.

LAKE HURON

Ontario

Nottawasaga River—Chinook and coho salmon, fall through spring steelhead, lake-run browns.

Access: Wasaga Beach Provencal Park, Baxter.

Beaver River—Fall through spring steelhead, lake-run browns.

Access: Thornbury Dam below Kimberly.

This silvery coho fell for a pink scud pattern in early September on the St. Joseph River.

Bighead River—Chinook salmon, fall through spring steelhead, lake-run browns.
Access: St. Vincent Township below and above to the branches.

Maitland River—Chinook and coho salmon, fall through spring steelhead, lake-run browns.
Access: Below Highway 21 and upstream to Wingham.

Saugeen River—Chinook salmon; fall, winter, spring, and summer steelhead; lake-run browns.
Access: Denny's Dam, Fisherman's Park, First Island, Graveyard Pool.

Michigan

Rifle River—Chinook salmon, fall through spring steelhead, lake-run browns.
Access: M-55, County Roads 18, 16, 19.

AuSable River—Chinook and coho salmon, fall through spring steelhead, lake-run browns.
Access: Below Foote Dam, Whirlpool Road.

Ocqueoc River—Chinook salmon, fall through spring steelhead, lake-run browns.
Access: Oqueoc Falls Dam.

LAKE MICHIGAN

Wisconsin

Kewaunee River—Chinook and coho salmon; fall, winter, spring, and summer steelhead; lake-run browns, splake.

Access: Highway F downstream to Highway C, Clyde's Hill Bridge to 3rd Highway C crossing.

Oconto River—Chinook and coho salmon; fall, winter, spring, and summer steelhead; lake-run browns.

Access: Dam at Stiles, Highway 41, Highway 141 bridge.

Peshtigo River—Chinook and coho salmon, fall through spring steelhead, lake-run browns.

Access: Peshtigo Dam, Highway 41.

Milwaukee River—Chinook and coho salmon; fall, winter, spring, and summer steelhead; lake-run browns.

Access: Second Dam at Grafter down, Kletzach Park to North Avenue Dam.

Steelhead often follow spawning salmon upriver to feed on their eggs. This fall fish spewed out a handful of eggs while being released.

Sheboygan River—Chinook and coho salmon; fall, winter, spring; and summer steelhead; lake-run browns.

Access: Highway PP, Black Wolf Run Golf Course, Kohler Estate.

Root River—Chinook and coho salmon; fall, winter, spring, and summer steelhead; lake-run browns.

Access: Horlick Dam, Lincoln Park.

Indiana

Little Calumet River—Chinook and coho salmon; fall, winter, spring, and especially summer Skamania steelhead; lake-run browns.

Access: Main Gate Bethlehem Steel Access, Route 20, Heron Rookery.

Salt Creek—Chinook and coho salmon; fall, winter, spring, and especially summer Skamania steelhead.

Access: Imagination Glen, Route 20, Joliett Road, Valporaiso.

Trail Creek—Chinook and coho salmon; fall, winter, spring, and especially summer Skamania steelhead; lake-run browns.

Access: Friendship Gardens, Route 20, Johnson Road, Creek Ridge Park.

Michigan

St. Joseph River—Chinook and coho salmon; fall, winter, and spring steelhead, especially summer Skamania steelhead; lake-run browns.

Access: Pipestone Creek, Lemon Creek, Sportsman's Club, Berrien Springs, Dowagiac Creek, Niles.

Grand River—Chinook and coho salmon, fall through spring steelhead, lake-run browns, lake trout.

Access: Sixth Street Dam, Rogue River, Prairie Creek, Lansing Dam.

Muskegon River—Chinook and coho salmon, fall through spring steelhead—especially winter steelhead—lake-run browns.

Access: Croton Dam, Pine Avenue, Thornapple, Henning Park, Bridgeton, Maple Island, North Causeway/Muskegon.

White River—Chinook and coho salmon, fall through spring steelhead, lake-run browns.

Access: Hesperia Dam, Garfield Road, Podunk, Pines Point, North Branch.

Pere Marquette River—Chinook and coho salmon, fall through spring steelhead, lake-run browns.

Access: 7 miles of flies-only, catch-and-release water; Rainbow Rapids; South Branch Bridge; Walhalla; Indian Bridge.

Little Manistee River—Chinook and coho salmon, fall through spring steelhead, lake-run browns.

Access: 6 to 9 mile road area.

Big Manistee—Chinook and coho salmon; fall, winter, spring, and summer Skamania steelhead; lake-run browns.

Access: Tippy Dam, High Bridge, Bear Creek.

Betsie River—Chinook and coho salmon; fall, winter, and spring steelhead; lake-run browns.
Access: Homestead Dam, below U.S. 31.
Platte River—Coho salmon; fall, winter, and spring steelhead; lake-run browns.
Access: M-22, Haze Road.
Carp River—Chinook salmon, fall through spring steelhead, lake-run browns.
Access: M-123, Ozark Road.

LAKE ERIE

Ontario

Grand River—Fall, winter, spring, and a late-summer run of steelhead.
Access: Below Paris downstream to mouth, Whitman's Creek.

Ohio

Rocky River—Fall, winter, and spring steelhead.
Access: Cleveland Metro Park System, Morely Rockcliff, Horse and Cedar Point Fords, Valley Parkway, and Brookpark Roads.
Grand River—Fall, winter, and spring steelhead.
Access: County Road 535, Painsville City Park, Indian Point Metro Park.
Chagrin River—Fall, winter, and spring steelhead.
Access: Woodland City Park, Daniel's Park, Chagrin River Park.

A bright coho salmon caught in the surf.

Conneaut Creek—Fall, winter, and spring steelhead.
Access: Old Main Road, Route 7, and at State, Kinsbury, Horton, and Wetmore Roads.

Pennsylvania

Elk Creek—Fall, winter, and spring steelhead.
Access: Whitman's, Tamery, and Sterrolania Roads; Routes 5 and 20; Guard Bois Park.
Walnut Creek—Fall, winter, and spring steelhead.
Access: Routes 5 and 20, Old Route 832, Manchester Road down, Zimmerly Road.

New York

Cattaraugus Creek—Chinook salmon; lake-run browns; and fall, winter, and spring steelhead. (Note: Especially early-running fall steelhead.)
Access: Gowanda, Zoar Valley, Indian Reservations, Gravel pits (above and below I-90), Routes 5 and 20, 438, Clear Creek, Taylor Hollow Road.
New York/Ontario's Niagara River—Chinook and coho salmon, lake trout, lake-run brown trout, fall, winter, and spring steelhead.
Access: U.S.—Whirlpool and Devil's Hole Park, Art Park, Niagara Bar. Canada—Niagara Parkway, Queenstown sand docks, Canadian Hydro Plant.

LAKE ONTARIO

Ontario

Credit River—Chinook and coho salmon, lake trout, lake-run browns, Atlantic salmon, fall, winter, and spring steelhead.

Access—Mississauga's Erindale Park, Highway J to QEW.

Wilmot Creek—Chinook salmon; lake-run browns; fall, winter, and spring steelhead; Atlantic salmon.

Access: Highway 2 below and above.

Ganaraska River—Chinook salmon, lake-run browns, fall, winter, and especially spring steelhead.

Access: Corbett Dam, upstream through the valley. (Note: Many posted and private roads. Ask for permission before entering.)

New York

Oak Orchard Creek—Chinook and coho salmon, especially lake-run browns, lake trout, Atlantic salmon, fall, winter, spring, and summer Skamania steelhead.

Access: Below Burt Dam.

Genesee River—Chinook and coho salmon, lake-run browns, lake trout, fall, spring, and especially winter steelhead.

Access: Lower falls off of Seth Green Drive.

Oswego River—Chinook, coho, lake-run browns, fall, winter, and spring steelhead.

Access: Varick Dam and below.

Salmon River—Chinook and coho salmon, Atlantic salmon, lake-run browns, lake trout, fall, winter, spring, and summer Skamania steelhead.

Access: Flies-only waters above Altmar; School-house, Trestle, and Compactor Pools; Pineville, Route 2A, Pulaski and Douglaston Waters.

North and South Sandy Creeks—Chinook and Atlantic salmon, lake-run browns, fall, winter, and spring steelhead.

Access: Ellisburg, Route 193, and Woodinville.

Black River—Chinook, coho, and Atlantic salmon, lake-run browns, lake trout, fall, winter, spring, and summer Skamania steelhead.

Access: Dexter Dam, Glenn Park, Watertown.

This stunning fresh-run steelhead is about to be released back into Michigan's lower Muskegon River.

FINAL THOUGHTS

While climatic changes, such as global warming and other environmental factors continue to affect the ecosystem of the Great Lakes, one thing is certain: We will have one of the greatest salmonid fisheries in the world for years to come. First, there must be deep, cold, clear water—food rich—and rivers with a magnificent diversity in character. Add a century of tradition and passion by salmon/steelhead anglers and fisheries managers, and what you have is a piscatorial landmark. It embodies the proud lifestyle and rugged, hard-working mentality of the natives, early settlers, and immigrants of the Industrial Revolution's melting pot. Cities like Buffalo, Toronto, Cleveland, Chicago, Muskegon, and Manistee, along with Milwaukee, Duluth, Thunder Bay, and Sault Ste. Marie, have toiled through economic hard times and industrial water pollution, only to see the Great Lakes cleaner and their economies healthier than ever before.

Exotic biological invaders, brought in from the ballast of ocean-going freighters, are changing and threatening our inland seas. Zebra and Quaga mussels, gobies, ruffees, exotic shrimp, etc. are threatening the indigenous balance of food forms that were a staple of the Great Lakes for hundreds, even thousands, of years. Similar changes are occurring in the Atlantic and Pacific Oceans, where salmon and steelhead survival is in jeopardy. Yet, there is a silver lining to all this. Our fishery is strong. We have an awakening of a new age of anglers. They are the guardians and protectors—passionate lovers—of our Great Lakes heritage. As their ranks swell, so will their vision to promote good fisheries management. This is essential, because what we are doing is for the long-term good—not just short term micro-management to appease harvesting charter-boat fleets. This leaves us with our pledge—our credo—on how we'll make the Great Lakes a better place to fish.

Respect each fish as a gift from God. Treat the rivers as partners in the exhilarating experience of fly fishing for salmonids. The massive numbers of salmon and steelhead caught over the past decades in our fishery will be our death knell. This only fuels our unchecked, distorted, and greedy appetite for more hook-ups and magic numbers of fish, which leads to

A deep scarlet sunset above Lake Michigan's Sleeping Bear Dunes.

shamefully rude streamside behavior. What will eventually result is a total collapse of the fishery, not to mention degrading ethical respect for the resource, other anglers, charter guides, and fisheries managers.

Learn to enjoy each angling outing as a special experience, the gift of a healthy and sound Great Lakes ecosystem. Each time you smile, are courteous, release a fish, pick up streamside trash, and share your angling knowledge and experiences with a fellow fisherman, you'll contribute to the legacy. By doing so, you will continue to enjoy our sport and grow into a master fly angler, which is a process you will cherish for a lifetime.

If all anglers learn to respect the extraordinary Great Lakes fishery, it will only get better with time.

INDEX